Good-Bye
FEAR

Dear Karen +
Charles & Blair
Phil 1:6

GOD'S ANTIDOTE TO FEAR

BETTY BLAIR

Goodbye Fear

Published by WP Publishing
Graphics & Printing by Workin' Perkins
www.workinperkins.com

ACKNOWLEDGEMENTS

My very special thanks —

To Bobbie Moore, for her untiring effort and those hours typing the manuscript so willingly,

To Dick Newman, for his journalistic mind and his encouragement to pursue this project,

To Keith Strawn, for his creative assistance with the cover design,

To Judy Stonecipher, for her excellent editing expertise,

And to my husband, Charles, whom I can always count on to say, "Go for it!"

To my husband
Charles,
Whose life and faith
continually
challenge
mine.

PROLOGUE

No one needed to tell me. Just a few moments in that hospital room, I sensed it. The body language – from her drawing imaginary lines on the bedcover to the nervous laugh in her conversation – it was evident. She was frightened! Tomorrow, she was scheduled for surgery – brain surgery.

What could I say? How should I pray?
What could I do to bring some sense of peace and hope to this dear one?
"Give me the words, Lord."

This scene happened more than once in my fifty-one years as a pastor's wife. Not always was it a hospital room; perhaps it was in a church pew or over a cup of coffee, but the scene was the same. Listening to an aching heart, seeing them face the crucible of their life, whether it was divorce or cancer – wishing that I possessed the power to save and heal or to somehow "fix it."

Realizing more and more, that it is only God who can do this. Truly, the greatest *"Balm in Gilead"* to comfort and heal is found in the words and promises which are spoken by God Himself.

While searching for those special words of encouragement, I found in the Scripture many verses about fear and selected just a few and called them my seven *"fear nots."* Very often, I included these in my notes to those in such circumstances. Almost always, the response was:

"Thank you for those *'fear nots'* – they really helped me."

My study showed me that the *fear factor* is something we face every day of our lives, and we are not alone – it is universal! But God has given us a solution and a promise for every situation. He has not left us alone to deal with life and its problems. He wants to be more than a "bridge over troubled waters"– rather, He wants to be the *pathway through them!*

My prayer is that you will let the truth of these words warm your heart. Learn from them. Grow with them. Share them with others and watch what happens. Not only will you be blessed, but *you will be a blessing!*

CONT E N T S

Part One

FACING FEAR

"For thus the Lord spoke to me with mighty power and instructed me not to walk in the way of this people, saying, 'You are not to say, "It is a conspiracy!"'

"And you are not to fear what they fear or be in dread of it. It is the Lord of hosts whom you should regard as holy. And He shall be your fear. And He shall be your dread. Then He shall become a sanctuary." Isaiah 8:12-14

"Be strong and courageous, do not be afraid or tremble at them, for the Lord your God is the one who goes with you. He will not fail you or forsake you."

"And the Lord is the one who goes ahead of you; He will be with you. He will not fail you or forsake you. Do not fear or be dismayed."

Deuteronomy 31:6, 8

"I cried unto the Lord

with my voice,

And He heard me From

His holy hill."

Psalm 3:4

1
THE CRY

"Oh, MY GOD!"

That's all that would come out of our mouths

From the fleeing crowds on the streets of New York to the stunned viewer miles away, the response was the same. Whether it was an exclamation or a prayer, it undoubtedly must have been the most uttered phrase heard throughout the world on that fateful day.

Certainly it was the one cry heard over and over again as we viewed that dreadful tragedy of September 11.

It was unbelief. It was shock. It was fear — all rolled together in one big heavy blow that left your head reeling and your heart hurting with every breath.

Not one, but two of the tallest skyscrapers in New York – the World Trade Center, had been targeted and hit by separate hijacked commercial aircraft, sending an inferno of flames billowing skyward and finally causing them to plummet to the ground like a child's tinker-toys.

Surely, this was a T.V. movie production – it couldn't be real. It was too awful!

My heart stood still. My mind couldn't absorb it all. I was immobilized. That scene on television kept me transfixed for hours. I wanted to cry, but it hurt too much. I just sat there and ached from the inside out.

We had never experienced before – our homeland, our shores, attacked without warning.

Who could have done such a thing?

How was it even possible in our great nation?

The headlines of the morning newspaper cried out:

AN EPIDEMIC OF FEAR [1]

My heart skipped a beat and my mind raced…thinking, "This is really WAR! – the first in decades – but not like any war I've ever known. It's diabolical. It's cunning. They're trying to destroy us from within. It's not just about killing bodies, but also a scheme to destroy the mind, soul and spirit of a whole nation. The plot seemed straight from the pits of hell! It had the 'fingerprints of Satan' all over it!"

The Wall Street Journal, October 19, 2001 reported: "Terrorism is not specifically designed to kill people or damage property…but rather to destroy our common faith in the mundane world, instilling fear and dread, and destroying a people's sense of the routine as a haven from turmoil.

As fear of terrorism mounts across the nation, many Americans are suddenly examining life's most banal routines, seeking to avoid invisible enemies and invisible weapons. People are doing anything 'to get one iota of control,' says

Ross, director of Ross Center for Anxiety & Related Disorders in Washington, D.C. Self-preservation enters into decisions people used to think nothing about:

Bottled water or Dr. Pepper?

> Stairs or elevator?

> > Cereal packaged before September 11 or after?

Only crazy people used to think that way.
Now, you're not so surprised." [2]

The clinical word for fear is "phoebe" from which we get the word *phobia*. It is defined as a panic that grips a person causing him to run away, be alarmed, scared, frightened, dismayed or filled with dread.

Actually, there are two kinds of fears – "godly fear," which is always constructive, "ungodly fear," which is always destructive.

The word itself occurs over 355 times in the Bible in the form of a noun, not to mention numerous other forms of the word such as fearful, afraid, anxious, alarmed, frightened, terrified and a host of others.

From those first recorded words of Adam uttered in the garden, *"I heard Your voice and I was afraid."* to the last pages of Revelation, we see and hear the pathos that accompanies this little four-letter word.

As we look back on that dreadful experience of September 11, we discover a very powerful principle:

MEN IN DEEP DISTRESS DO AND ALWAYS WILL CRY OUT TO GOD!

When some overwhelming need comes upon them, their impulse is still to pray. Sometimes a crisis or personal danger loosens this hidden impulse. "I hadn't prayed in ten years," a man exclaimed when his train had just escaped a wreck; "but I prayed then." A crushing responsibility will make men pray almost in spite of themselves.

One great writer argues: "Can it be that all men, in all ages and all lands, have been engaged in talking forever to a silent world from which no answer comes?

If we can be sure of anything, it is this---that wherever a human function has persisted, unwearied by time, uncrushed by disappointment, rising to its noblest form and finest use in the noblest and finest souls, that function corresponds with reality.

> Hunger could never have persisted without food,
>> nor breathing without air,
>>> nor intellectual life without truth,
>>>> nor prayer without God." [3]

In the Scripture we read of those who cried out to God in their despair:

JONAH

*"**I cried out to** the Lord because of my affliction."*
"When my soul fainted within me, I remembered the Lord."

JONAH 2:2, 7 NKJ

ISRAEL

*"Then the children of Israel groaned because of the bondage, and they **cried out**; and their cry came up to God because of the bondage."*

EXODUS 2:23 NKJ

DAVID

*"In my distress I called upon the Lord, and **cried out** to my God;"*

PSALMS 18:6a NKJ

*"I **cry out** with my whole heart, Hear me, O Lord!"*

*"I **cry out** to You.... Save me..."*

PSALMS119:145, 146 NKJ

But the glorious good news is — when we cry out to God with a whole heart, the Lord hears, listens and responds. Note the latter part of these same verses:

JONAH

*"And **He answered me**."*

JONAH 2:2b

ISRAEL

*"So God heard their groaning, and God remembered His covenant with Abraham, with Isaac, and with Jacob. And God looked upon the children of Israel, and **God acknowledged them**."*

EXODUS 2:24, NKJ

DAVID

*"He **heard my voice** from His temple, and my cry came before Him, even to His ears."*

PSALMS 18:6b, NKJ

*"And **He heard me** from His holy hill."*

PSALMS 3:4, NKJ

*"I sought the Lord, and **He heard me,** And delivered me from all my fears."*

PSALMS 34:4, NKJ

The prophet Isaiah gives us a truth and a principle that is found and confirmed throughout the whole of the Scripture:

*"Then you shall call and the **Lord will answer**; You shall cry, and He will say, 'Here I am'."*

ISAIAH 58:9, NKJ

GOD'S ANSWER

"Save me" are the words that usually accompany *"THE CRY."* If the phrase is not literally spoken, it is most certainly present in our minds. In Hebrew the word is *"YASHA."* It is found more than 200 times throughout the Old Testament.

And herein we find a most thrilling truth:

God chose a form of this verb to be His Son's name. "YESHUA," meaning *"He shall save."* It is a one-word description of God's response to the needs of humanity. It was the shining message given by the angels –

To MARY

> *"He shall **save** His people from their sins."*
>
> MATTHEW 1:21, KJ

> *"My soul magnifies the Lord, and my spirit has rejoiced in God my **Savior**."*
>
> LUKE 1:46, NKJ

To SHEPHERDS

> *"For there is born to you this day in the city of David **a Savior**, who is Christ the Lord."*
>
> LUKE 2:11, NKJ

To JOHN

> *"...and we know that this is indeed the Christ, the **Savior** of the world."*
>
> JOHN 4:42, NKJ

"THE CRY" may begin as an erratic, instinctive impulse, but it may and will grow to be a dependable and all-saving power. It is the cry that God waits to hear from your heart and mine, so that He may become **our Savior**!

One promise I can make to you unequivocally. The day you decide to *cry out* to God with all your heart will be the day of *new beginnings* in your life. For once you have dealings with God, you can never be the same. You might say it's like being *"born again!"*

2
THE QUESTION

It was a warm summer Sunday evening; we were at church with our grandson, Marrles and his little family.

Suddenly the sirens began to sound a shrill alarm. The imminent news :

A TORNADO WATCH WAS IN EFFECT.

One had touched down nearby and everyone was ordered to evacuate to the lowest part of the building.

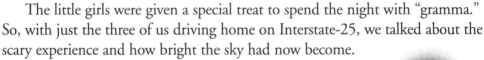

Marrles Moore and daughter Blair

With children in tow (Blair and Morgan) we huddled on the floor of the lower auditorium waiting for the signal that the storm had passed over and everything was safe.

The little girls were given a special treat to spend the night with "gramma." So, with just the three of us driving home on Interstate-25, we talked about the scary experience and how bright the sky had now become.

Then from the back seat, I heard a little voice:

"Gramma, why does God let tornados happen?"

A long pause…I was thinking.

"Well, Blair, it's like this."

I began to wax eloquent on the different kinds of cloud formations, from the beautiful, fluffy "cumulus" to the dark ominous "nimbus"– which ones had rain, which had hail, and which were just pretty to watch as they float by. And then how tornados result when hot and cold air masses collide and form a black, funnel-shaped finger that destroys everything in its path – trees, trains, bridges, buildings – all swept away like paper dolls.

They listened quietly. I thought I was brilliant.

Morgan & Blair

About an hour later we were having a little snack around the kitchen table, when Blair blurted out:

"Gramma, I didn't ask *how*…I asked *why?*"

Silence…Now the ball was in my court.

So I said: "Let's let Grandpa answer that one – he's the theologian in this family."

Blair had epitomized the age-old question we all ask.

WHY?

Why does a good God let bad things happen?

Why do bad things happen to good people?

Why must all our hopes and dreams be blasted?

That is one of the first questions we ask when tragedy strikes.
And there is no easy answer. But there are answers.

God has given us a Book, sometimes appropriately called *"The Manufacturer's Hand-book,"* which is a guide to us for life and living; it is called the Bible. It gives us all we need to know about the past and the future, as well as the essentials for a fruitful life here on earth.

> *"Why are ye fearful?"*
> *Matthew 8:26*

It is history in living color — people demonstrating principles.

It is *"His story"* of God and man's relationship.

It tells how sin came into this one-time happy, peaceful world and of the battle between good and evil. There are stories of man's struggles and his search for God.

And finally, God's provision for man's greatest need – redemption.

SOMETIMES GOD

As we read the Bible, we find that God often allows adversity for a specific reason – as a warning. Throughout the Old Testament God was fairly consistent in punishing evil and rewarding good. He used the sword, famine and pestilence over and over again. It usually involved warning and was always tied to repentance. He wanted to model His chosen nation to demonstrate to the heathen world the great power and blessings that come from serving the one true God – Jehovah.

But, in the age of "grace" it seems God is not so quick to judge. Instead He allows
the wheat and the chaff to grow up together,
the rain to fall on the just and the unjust,
the wicked to prosper and the godly to hurt.

Clearly, then, pain and suffering are part of our planet and Christians are
not exempt.

If God were to punish every sin with suffering and reward every good deed with
pleasure, then our goodness would be tainted with selfish motives. We would love
Him for the wrong reasons. What He desires is that we commit ourselves to Him,
not to our own feelings and not only for rewards.

SOMETIMES SATAN

In the book of Job we see:

Satan as the perpetrator....*but God as the "Administrator,"*

Satan as the instigator,...*but God as the "Navigator."*

> *"Shall we
indeed accept
good from God
and not accept
adversity?"*
>
> *Job 2:10, NKJ*

What Satan began, God finished!

And in doing so, God gives to us certain principles:

1) God is sovereign. We cannot understand His workings by rational
thinking alone; faith must rest in God's love and our knowledge of Him.

2) We understand ourselves and our lives in direct relation to our
understanding of the character and workings of God.

3) In times of tragedy we face the temptation of making God our *adversary*
instead of *our advocate.*

4) The struggle of faith is a personal one. We each enter the crucible of life
alone; we must test the mettle of our faith in God against uncontrollable
forces and win our individual victories. There will be times when family
and friends may be taken from us and we must stand alone.

JOB (SPIRIT FILLED BIBLE) [1]

God could have placed us in an environment free from pain, but think what
puny Christians we would be! Somehow, He uses life with its sorrows and tears
to be a part of our own soul-making.

If there were no dangers or difficulties in life, there would be no fear; but then we would never know about

COURAGE…or FAITH…or HOPE…or TRUST.

He wants us to cleave to Him, as Job did, even when we have every reason to deny Him – to fall into His loving arms, and cling to Him even when we can't understand.

When we begin to search for answers, an amazing thing happens. We not only find answers, but we find the ONE who has the answers. And in our seeking, we come to know Him and a relationship begins.

> *"Thus saith the Lord, Let not the wise man glory in his wisdom, neither let the mighty man glory in his might, let not the rich man glory in his riches: But let him that glorieth glory in this, that he understandeth and knoweth Me…"*
>
> JEREMIAH 9:23, KJ

God's ultimate desire is a relationship with us. He is always calling, seeking, wooing from the first pages of His "Book" to the last:

> *"Adam, where art thou?"*
>
> GENESIS 3:9, KJ

> *"…the Spirit and the bride say, 'Come'…whosoever will, let him take of the water of life freely."*
>
> REVELATION 22:17, KJ

And God promises:

> *"And you will seek Me and find Me, when you search for Me with all your heart. 'And I will be found by you,' declares the Lord…"*
>
> JEREMIAH 29:13,14

Then, in our search for Him, we discover: His ways are higher than our ways, and His thoughts higher than our thoughts… Isaiah 55: 8, 9.

Soon our understanding is opened to seeing life from God's perspective. Tragedies, trials, difficulties and problems somehow "fit" into the picture – the tapestry of our lives.

As J. I. Packer says, "losses and crosses pale into insignificance compared to the knowledge of God which we have gained." [2]

And, of course, one of God's ways is to take that which is meant for *evil* and out of it bring *good*. That is, of all things, miraculous – but God delights in doing it!' The Bible is full of stories proving that *only God* possesses that *Divine alchemy* which can bring:

GOOD OUT OF EVIL
STRENGTH OUT OF WEAKNESS
JOY OUT OF SORROW
PEACE IN MIDST OF PAIN
FAITH IN PLACE OF DOUBT
COURAGE IN PLACE OF FEAR
LOVE OVER HATE
LIFE OUT OF DEATH

EXAMPLES

1) GOOD OUT OF EVIL:

JOSEPH

"And as for you, you meant evil against me, but God meant it for good in order to bring about this present result, to preserve many people alive.

So therefore, do not be afraid; I will provide for you and your little ones."
GENESIS 50: 20, 21

MOSES

"So they appointed taskmasters over them to afflict them with hard labor... commanded every son cast into the Nile..."
EXODUS 1:11, 22

...and the child grew...and he became her son. And she named him Moses."
EXODUS 2:10

ISRAEL

"I am the Lord, and I will bring you out from under the burdens of the Egyptians, and I will deliver you from their bondage.

…Then I will take you for My people, and I will be your God; and you shall know that I am the Lord your God, who brought you out from under the burdens of the Egyptians.

And I will bring you to the land which I swore to give to Abraham, Isaac, and Jacob, and I will give it to you for a possession; I am the Lord."

EXODUS 6: 6-8

DAVID

"And the Philistine cursed David by his gods…Come to me, and I will give your flesh to the birds of the sky and the beasts of the field.

Then David said to the Philistine, 'You come to me with a sword, a spear, and a javelin, but I come to you in the name of the Lord of Hosts, the God of the armies of Israel, whom you have taunted.

This day the Lord will deliver you up into my hands…that all the earth may know that there is a God in Israel."

I SAMUEL 17:43B-46

SAUL

"Now Saul, still breathing threats and murder against the disciples of the Lord,…as he journeyed, he was approaching Damascus, and suddenly a light from heaven flashed around him; and he fell to the ground and heard a voice saying to him, 'Saul, Saul, Why are you persecuting Me?'

And he said, 'Who art Thou, Lord?' And He said, 'I am Jesus whom you are persecuting,…rise, enter the city, and it shall be told you what you must do.'"

ACTS 9:1-6

"The Lord said to him, 'Go, for he is a chosen instrument of Mine, to bear My name before the Gentiles and kings and the sons of Israel; for I will show him how much he must suffer for My name's sake.'"

ACTS 9:15, 16

In each of these instances, God took that which was evil and out of it brought something good!

2) STRENGTH OUT OF WEAKNESS

PAUL

"... There was given me a thorn in the flesh, a messenger of Satan to buffet me – to keep me from exalting myself!

*Concerning this I entreated the Lord three times that it might depart from me. And He has said to me, 'My grace is sufficient for you, **for power is perfected in weakness.'** Most gladly, therefore, I will rather boast about my weaknesses, that the power of Christ may dwell in me. Therefore I am well content with weaknesses, with insults, with distresses, with persecutions, with difficulties, for Christ's sake; for when I am **weak,** then I am **strong.**"*

II CORINTHIANS 12:7-10

Again, out of weakness, God demonstrated His unlimited power and strength!

3) JOY IN FACE OF SORROW

APOSTLES

"...they flogged them and ordered them to speak no more in the name of Jesus, and then released them.

*So they went on their way from the presence of the Council, **rejoicing** that they had been considered worthy to suffer shame for His name. And every day they kept right on teaching and preaching Jesus as the Christ."*

ACTS 5: 40-42

PAUL & SILAS

"And the crowd rose up together against them, and the chief magistrates tore their robes off them, and proceeded to order them to be beaten with rods.

And when they had inflicted many blows upon them, they threw them into prison, commanding the jailer to guard them securely; and he, having received such a command, threw them into the inner prison, and fastened their feet in stocks.

*But about midnight Paul and Silas were praying and **singing hymns of praise to God**,…and suddenly there came a great earthquake…"*

ACTS 16:22-26

*"As sorrowful, yet always **rejoicing**, as poor, yet making many rich, as having nothing, and yet possessing all things."*

II CORINTHIANS 6:10

How very true it is:

> *JOY IS NOT THE ABSENCE OF SUFFERING,*
> *BUT THE PRESENCE OF CHRIST!*

4) PEACE IN THE MIDST OF PAIN

STEPHEN

"…they began gnashing their teeth at him. But being full of the Holy Spirit, he gazed intently into heaven and saw the glory of God, and Jesus standing at the right hand of God;…But they cried out with a loud voice and covered their ears, and they rushed upon him with one impulse. And when they had driven him out of the city, they began stoning him…And falling on his knees, he cried out with a loud voice, 'Lord do not hold this sin against them!' And having said this, he fell asleep."

ACTS 7: 54, 55, 58, 60

JESUS

*"**Peace** I leave with you; My **peace** I give unto you; not as the world gives, do I give to you. Let not your heart be troubled, nor let it be fearful."*

JOHN 14:27

*"These things I have spoken to you, that in Me you may have **peace**. In the world you have tribulation, but take courage; I have overcome the world."*

JOHN 16:33

5) FAITH IN PLACE OF DOUBT

ABRAHAM

*"By **faith** Abraham, when he was called, obeyed by going out to a place which he was to receive for an inheritance; and he went out, not knowing where he was going.*

*By **faith** he lived as an alien in the land of promise, as in a foreign land, dwelling in tents with Isaac and Jacob, fellow-heirs of the same promise;*

For he was looking for the city which has foundations, whose architect and builder is God."

HEBREWS 11:8-10

*"By **faith** Abraham, when he was tested, offered up Isaac; and he who had received the promises was offering up his only begotten son;...He considered that God is able to raise men even from the dead; from which he also received him back as a type."*

HEBREWS 11:17, 19

MOSES

*"By **faith**, Moses, when he had grown up, refused to be called the son of Pharaoh's daughter; choosing rather to endure ill-treatment with the people of God, than to enjoy the passing pleasures of sin; considering the reproach of Christ greater riches than the treasures of Egypt; for he was looking to the reward."*

HEBREWS 11:24-26

DAVID

"David said moreover, 'The Lord that delivered me out of the paw of the lion, and out of the paw of the bear, he will deliver me out of the hand of this Philistine. And Saul said to David, 'Go, and the Lord be with thee.'"

I SAMUEL 17:37 KJ

6) COURAGE IN PLACE OF FEAR

JOSHUA

"Have I not commanded you? Be strong and **courageous**! Do not tremble or be dismayed, for the Lord your God is with you wherever you go."

JOSHUA 1:9

"Do not fear them, for I have given them into your hands; not one of them shall stand before you."

"And there was no day like that before it or after it, when the Lord listened to the voice of a man; for the Lord fought for Israel."

JOSHUA 10:8, 14

CALEB

"Now therefore give me this mountain, whereof the Lord spake in that day; for thou heardest in that day how the Anakim were there, and that the cities were great and fenced: if so be the Lord will be with me, then I **shall be able** to drive them out, as the Lord said."

JOSHUA 14:12 KJ

DAVID

"And David said to Saul, Let no man's heart fail because of him; thy servant **will go** and **fight** with this Philistine."

I SAMUEL 17:32, KJ

Three CAPTIVES

"Shadrach, Meshach, and Abednego, answered and said to the king, 'O Nebuchadnezzar, we are not careful to answer thee in this matter.

If it be so, our God whom we serve is able **to deliver** us from the burning fiery furnace...'"

DANIEL 3:16.17, KJ

DANIEL

"Now when Daniel knew that the writing was signed, he went into his house; and his windows being open in his chamber toward Jerusalem, he **kneeled upon his knees three times a day**, and **prayed**, and **gave thanks** before his God, as he did aforetime."

DANIEL 6:10, KJ

7) **LOVE OVER HATE**

DAVID

"Behold, this day your eyes have seen that the Lord had given you today into my hand in the cave, and some said to kill you, but my eye had pity on you; and I said, 'I **will not stretch out my hand against my lord,** for he is the Lord's anointed.'"

"And he (Saul) said to David, 'You are more righteous than I; for you have dealt well with me, while I have dealt wickedly with you.'"

I SAMUEL 24: 10, 17

JOSEPH

"And now do not be grieved or angry with yourselves, because you sold me here; for God sent me before you to preserve life.

And **he kissed all his brothers and wept on them**, and afterward his brothers talked with him."

GENESIS 45: 5, 15

PAUL

"To this present hour we are both hungry and thirsty, and are poorly clothed, and are roughly treated, and are homeless; and we toil, working with our own hands; when we are reviled, we **bless**; when we are persecuted, we **endure**; when we are slandered, we try to **conciliate**; we have become as the scum of the world, the dregs of all things, even until now."

I CORINTHIANS 4:11-13

8) LIFE OUT OF DEATH

PAUL

"But we have this treasure in earthen vessels, that the surpassing greatness of the power may be of God and not from ourselves;

*We are afflicted in every way, but not crushed; perplexed, but not despairing; persecuted, but not forsaken; struck down, but not destroyed; always carrying about in the body the dying of Jesus, that the **life of Jesus** also may be manifested in our body.....*

*So death works in us, but **life** in you."*

II CORINTHIANS 4:7-12

JESUS

*"For whosoever will save his life shall lose it: but whosoever will lose his life for My sake, the same shall **save** it."*

LUKE 9: 24, KJ

*"Verily, verily, I say unto you, Except a corn of wheat fall into the ground and die, it abideth alone: but if it die, it **bringeth forth much fruit**."*

JOHN 12:24 KJ

*"For ye are dead, and your life is hid with Christ in God. When Christ, who is our **life**, shall appear, then shall ye also appear with him in glory."*

COLOSSIANS 3: 3, 4 KJ

*"I am he that liveth, and was dead; and, behold, I am **alive** for evermore, Amen; and **have the keys** of hell and of death."*

REVELATION 1:18 KJ

GOD'S WAYS HIGHER
THAN MAN'S WAYS

1. God plans for eternity; man for time.

2. God the spiritual; man the material.

3. God consecrates Himself to the highest good of all; man to self-gratification.

4. God exalts thru humility; man thru self-exaltation.

5. God controls by love; man by force.

6. God wins respect by goodness; man by wealth and power.

7. God's program is carried on without outward show; man's by show and splendor.

8. God's way is to take no thought for the morrows; man's way is made up of constant worry, planning, and fretting.

9. God's way is to put away grudges and all bitterness; man's is to hold them and seek revenge.

10. God's way is to lend, hoping nothing in return; man's is not to lend without security and gain.

11. God's way is to judge not; man's is to judge.

12. God's way is to forgive 490 times; man's to forgive a few times, and only when necessary.

"*And there will be signs in
the sun, in the moon, and in the stars;
and on the earth distress of nations,
with perplexity . . . . . .
Men's hearts failing them from fear . . . .*"

Luke 21:25, 26

3
FEAR
The Bad Kind

There is a kind of fear that is fair. We call it fair because it is legitimate. It is justifiable. It is called *unholy* or *ungodly fear;* it is characteristic of the wicked and it is present in them because of sin. Genesis 3:10, 24

It seems apparent that this fear is that passion which is chiefly dominant in the breast of fallen man. Adam, before his fall, knew nothing of it; but after his transgression he fled from the face of God and hid himself amongst the trees of the garden because of his fear. Ever since, many or most appearances of God or angels have generated fear and so they have punctuated their appearance with the encouraging expression, *"Fear not."*

CONSCIENCE

God has placed within each one of us a little "monitor" called conscience; and even before we take a step…while we are still considering our way…that little voice will protest immediately and make us uneasy as to any thought or inclination which is unpleasing to Him.

Such activity of the conscience augments the anguish of a sinner. It is called *conviction* – and God is ever using this means to draw man to Himself.

It's a bit like the song we used to sing:
>"Love and marriage, Love and marriage,
>Go together, like a horse and carriage;

You can't have one, you can't have one,
You can't have one...without the other."

So it is with sin –
Sin and guilt go together –
You can't have one without the other.

And sometimes God uses frightening things to make a point!
Such as Mt. Sinai, when there were thunders and lightnings and a thick cloud and the voice of the trumpet exceeding loud, so that the people trembled! Exodus 19:16

And the earthquake when Paul and Silas prayed and sang in the Philippian jail. Acts 16:26

In the book of Job we get a glimpse of the way in which the wicked are punished and how his fears are all consuming. *"All around terrors frighten him, and harry him at every step."* Job 18:11

In other words, the terrors of man's own conscience haunt him wherever he goes; wherever he looks, it stares him in the face. He carries his own accuser, his own tormentor in his bosom. No wonder he flees when no one pursues. Proverbs 28:1

FEAR OF PUNISHMENT

Fear of future punishment is also an underlying factor; and of course, this is understandable when you remember how God dealt with those disobedient Israelites and the curses He sent to punish them.

"I will even appoint terror over you, wasting disease and fever which shall consume the eyes and cause sorrow of heart. And you shall sow your seed in vain, for your enemies shall eat it. I will set My face against you, and you shall be defeated by your enemies. Those who hate you shall reign over you, and you shall flee when no one pursues you. And after all this, if you do not obey Me, then I will punish you seven times more for your sins. I will break the pride of your power..."

LEVITICUS 26:16-18, NKJ

It is also interesting that more than once, God used the *sword, famine* and *pestilence* as a punishment to His people. Leviticus 26:25-26

Other severe warnings from God:

*"And among those nations you shall find no rest, nor shall the sole of your foot have a resting place; but there the Lord will give you a trembling heart, failing eyes, and anguish of soul Your life shall hang in doubt before you; you shall **fear** day and night, and have no assurance of life.*

*In the morning you shall say, 'Oh, that it were evening!' And at evening you shall say, 'Oh, that it were morning!' because of the **fear** which terrifies your heart, and because of the sight which your eyes see.*

And the Lord will take you back to Egypt in ships, by the way of which I said to you, 'You shall never see it again.' And there you shall be offered for sale to your enemies as male and female slaves, but no one will buy you."

DEUTERONOMY 28:65-68 NKJ

SEPTEMBER 11

Our hearts ache and we weep quietly when we hear the stories of the many victims and the devastated families who were left behind in the fiery tragedy of September 11. And of the many heroes whose stories will never be told.

Jeremiah records another tragic picture that will break your heart. The saddest part of this narrative is not simply the terrible loss of human life, but that, through it all, Israel found it so difficult to repent.

What breaks your heart is that —
    God is so good, and the people so disobedient,
    God is so benevolent, and the people so ungrateful,
    God is so patient, and the people so rebellious,
    God is so holy, and the people so blatantly sinful,
    God is so angry, and the people so blind,
    God is so merciful and forgiving, and the people so unrepentant,
    God is so faithful, and the people still redeemable.

In hind sight, we see the picture — and we weep.

THE STORY

Jerusalem was under siege.

Jeremiah was shut up in prison.

And God seemed far away.

In distress and confused about the meaning of God's providences, Jeremiah began to pray:

"Ah, Lord God! Behold, You have made the heavens and the earth by Your great power and outstretched arm. There is nothing too hard for You.

You show loving kindness to thousands, and repay the iniquity of the fathers into the bosom of their children after them — the Great, the Mighty God, whose name is the Lord of hosts.

You are great in counsel and mighty in work, for your eyes are open to all the ways of the sons of men, to give everyone according to his ways and according to the fruit of his doings of his doings.

You have set signs and wonders in the land of Egypt, to this day, and in Israel and among other men; and you have made Yourself a name, as it is this day.

You have brought Your people Israel out of the land of Egypt with signs and wonders, with a strong hand and an outstretched arm, and with great terror;

You have given them this land, of which You swore to their fathers to give them —'a land flowing with milk and honey.'

*And they came in and took possession of it, but they have not obeyed Your voice or walked in Your law. They have done nothing of all that You commanded them to do; therefore You have **caused all this calamity** to come upon them.*

*Look, the siege mounds! They have come to the city to take it; and the city has been given into the hand of the Chaldeans who fight against it, because of the **sword** and **famine** and **pestilence**. What You have spoken has happened; there You see it!"*

JEREMIAH 32:17-24 NKJ

The narrative continues throughout the whole chapter as God reiterates His heart cry for His people. His overtures are heard again and again, as He reaches out in love:

> *"I will gather them…bring them back…they shall be My people, and I will be their God; and I will give them one heart and one way, that they may* **fear Me** *forever, for their own good, and for the good of their children after them. And I will make an everlasting covenant with them that I will not turn away from doing them good; but I will put* **My fear** *in their hearts so that they will not depart from Me."*
>
> JEREMIAH 32:37-40 NKJ

Can you believe it? According to Jeremiah, God used his 3-fold punishment 15 times by *"sword, famine and pestilence"* to punish; it was part of the curse of Leviticus 26:25 for disobeying God. It reminds us of these sad words:

> *"My people are destroyed for lack of knowledge: Because you have rejected knowledge, I will also reject you from being priest for Me. Because you have forgotten the law of your God. I will also forget your children."*
>
> HOSEA 4:6 NKJ

No wonder Jeremiah was called "the prophet of tears."

The message of Jeremiah is relevant because it is timeless. **Sin must always be punished; but true repentance brings restoration!**

Our idolatry which consists of such things as wealth, talent or position is called by new names, but sin is the same…and the remedy is the same!

God calls for obedience to His commands in a pure covenantal relationship.

Sin requires *repentance* and *restoration*; but obedience leads to ***blessing*** and ***joy!***

No Fear Nots
For the Ungodly!

"The fear of the
Lord is a Fountain of Life."
Psalm 14:27

4
FEAR
The Good Kind

GOD IS THE AUTHOR

*"And I will give them one heart and one way, that they may **fear Me** always, for their own good, and for the good of their children after them. And I will make an everlasting covenant with them that I will not turn away from them, to do them good; and I will put the **fear of Me** in their hearts so that they will not turn away from Me."*

JEREMIAH 32:39, 40

GOD IS ALSO THE OBJECT

*"It is the Lord of hosts whom you should regard as holy. And He shall be your **fear**."*

ISAIAH 8:13a

"The fear of the Lord leads to life." Proverbs 19:23

THE ADVANTAGES OF

*"Better is a little with the **fear of the Lord**, than great treasure and turmoil with it."*

PROVERBS 15:16

*'The **fear of the Lord** leads to life, so that one may sleep satisfied, untouched by evil."*

PROVERBS 19:23

37

*"Although a sinner does evil a hundred times and may lengthen his life, still I know that it will be well for those who **fear God**, who **fear Him** openly."*
ECCLESIASTES. 8:12, 13

COMMANDED

Moses, knowing the tendencies of the people and the perils of idolatry, issued some clear charges to Israel, beginning with those related to the worship of God — particularly those in relation to the second commandment, about which God is, in a special manner, jealous.

*"You shall walk after the Lord your God and **fear Him**, and keep His commandments and obey His voice; you shall serve Him and hold fast to Him."*
DEUTERONOMY 13:4, NJK

Solomon, the man of wisdom, said that the wise individual chooses those things that have lasting value, which most often will *not* be chosen by the world's standards.

*"**Fear God** and keep His commandments. For this is man's all."*
ECCLESIASTES 12:13, NKJ

And Peter puts it simply, but succinctly:

*"Honor all People. Love the brotherhood. **Fear God.** Honor the king."*
I PETER 2:17, NKJ

WHY NECESSARY?

1) TO AVOID SIN

The deepest desire of God's heart was, and is, to have a people, a special people, who somehow reflect Him. In other words to be holy, *"set apart to Him and His purposes."* They would be distinguished in nature and character from the world, different in the way they think, act, and live. This difference would be visible and bring great glory to God.

However, there would need to be an intrinsic motivation; otherwise, this could never happen. Man is too prone to sin and needs help in order to understand and please God. So God issued the Ten Commandments giving us the principles that teach us how to live wisely and please God. Then He added a little "fireworks" to make a point! "Moses said to the people, 'Do not be afraid, God has come to test you, so that the *fear of God will be with you to keep you from sinning.*'" Exodus 20:20 NIV

> *"The fear*
> *of the Lord is to*
> *hate evil."*
> Proverbs 8:13

So the *fear of the Lord* is an essential "motivator" in **avoiding sin.** Likewise, it is active in the perfecting of holiness in our lives.

> *"Having therefore these promises, dearly beloved, let us cleanse ourselves from all filthiness of the flesh and spirit, perfecting holiness in the **fear of God.**"*
>
> II CORINTHIANS 7:1 KJ

2) FOUNDATIONAL TO OUR WORSHIP

> *"But as for me, I will come into Your house in the multitude of Your mercy; In fear of You I will **worship** toward Your holy temple."*
>
> PSALMS 5:7 NKJ

> *"God is greatly to be feared in the assembly of the saints, And to be **held in reverence** by all those around Him."*
>
> PSALMS 89:7 NKJ

David spent much time in private worship, praying often alone (Psalms 5: 2, 3) and yet was very constant and devout in his attendance to the sanctuary. We can be sure of this, his private worship in the closet undoubtedly prepared him doubly for public worship.

> *"Since we have a kingdom nothing can destroy, let us please God by serving Him with thankful hearts, and with **holy fear** and **awe.**"*
>
> HEBREWS 12:28 TLB

3) REASONS FOR DOING SO

God's Forgiveness

> "*But there is **forgiveness** with You. That You may be feared.*"
>
> Psalms 130:4 NKJ

God's Goodness

> *Only fear the Lord, and serve Him in truth with all your heart, for consider **what great things He has done for you.**"*
>
> I Samuel 12:24 NKJ

God's Greatness

> "*And now, Israel, what does the Lord your God require of you, but to fear the Lord your God, to walk in all His ways and to love Him, and to serve the Lord your God with all your heart and with all your soul…for **He is great** and **mighty** and the **awesome God** who does not show partiality nor take a bribe.*"
>
> Deuteronomy 10:12, 17

God's Wondrous Works

> "*for the Lord your God **dried up the waters** of the Jordan before you until you had crossed over, as the Lord your God **did to the Red Sea**, which He dried up before us until we had crossed over. That all peoples of the earth may know the hand of the Lord…that it is mighty, that you may fear the Lord your God forever.*"
>
> Joshua 4:23, 24 NKJ

God's Holiness

> "*Who shall not fear You, O Lord, and glorify Your name? For **You alone are holy**. For all nations shall come and worship before You. For Your judgments have been manifested.*"
>
> Revelation 15:4 NKJ

God's Judgments

> "*…saying with a loud voice, 'Fear God and give glory to Him, for the hour of **His judgment** has come; and worship Him who made heaven and earth, the sea and springs of water.'*"
>
> Revelation 14:7 NKJ

Righteous Gov't.

> *"The God of Israel said, 'The Rock of Israel spoke to me: He who rules over men must **be just, Ruling in the fear of God.**"*
>
> II Samuel 23:3 NKJ

4) BENEFITS OF GODLY FEAR
A Fountain of Life

> *" The fear of the Lord is a **fountain of life...**"*
>
> PROVERBS 14:27a

Sanctifying

> *The fear of the Lord is **clean**, enduring forever: the judgments of the Lord are true and righteous altogether."*
>
> Psalms 19:9 NKJ

Wisdom

> *"Behold, the fear of the Lord; that is **wisdom**: and to depart from evil is understanding."*
>
> Job 28:28 NKJ

Understand Scripture

> *"If you cry out for discernment, and lift up your voice for understanding... then you will **understand** the fear of the Lord and **find the knowledge of God.** For the Lord gives wisdom; from His mouth comes knowledge and understanding."*
>
> PROVERBS 2:3, 5-6 NKJ

Days Prolonged

> *"The fear of the Lord **prolongs** days, but the years of the wicked will be shortened."*
>
> PROVERBS 10:27 NKJ

5) GOD'S BLESSING ON GODLY FEAR
Accepted by God

> *"But in every nation whoever fears Him and works righteousness is **accepted** by Him."*
>
> ACTS 10:35 NKJ

Delights God

*"The Lord **takes pleasure** in those who fear Him."*

PSALMS 147:11 NKJ

Blessed by God

*"**Blessed** is the man who fears the Lord, who delights greatly in his commandments."*

PSALMS 112:1 NKJ

*"He will **bless** those who fear the Lord, both small and great."*

Psalms 115:13 NKJ

*"He will **fulfill the desire** of those who fear Him; He also will hear their cry and save them."*

Psalms 145:19 NKJ

*"You who fear the Lord, trust in the Lord; He is their **Help and their Shield.**"*

Psalms 115:11 NKJ

CONSPICUOUS INSTANCES OF THOSE WHO FEARED GOD:

Noah, in preparing the ark. Hebrews 11:7

Abraham, tested in offering his son, Isaac. Genesis 22:12

Jacob, in the vision of the ladder. Genesis 28:16, 17

Midwives of Egypt, in refusing to kill Hebrew children. Exodus 1:17, 21

Egyptians at the plague of thunder, hail and fire. Exodus 9:20

Nine and one-half tribes of Israel west of Jordan. Joshua 22:15-20

Phinehas, in turning away the anger of God at the time of the plague. Numbers 25:11

Obadiah, in sheltering 100 prophets against the wrath of Jezebel. I Kings 18:3,4

Jehoshaphat, in proclaiming a fast upon invasion by Ammonites and Moabites. 2 Chronicles 20:3

Nehemiah, in his reform. Nehemiah 5:15

Hanani, which qualified him to be ruler over Jerusalem. Nehemiah 7:2

Job, according to the testimony of Satan. Job 1:8

David, in meditation and prayers.   Psalms 5:7; 119:38

Hezekiah, in his treatment of the prophet Micah, who prophesied evil against Jerusalem. Jeremiah 26:19

Jonah, in the tempest. Jonah 1:9

The Jews, in obeying the voice of the Lord. Haggai 1:12

Levi, in receiving the covenant of life and peace. Haggai 1:5

The women at the sepulcher. Matthew 28:8

Cornelius, who feared God with all his house. Acts 10:2

And we might add to that list:

Simeon Routh, a just and devout man, who, with his whole house, feared God and served Him faithfully. I knew him as my grandpa Routh.

Simeon was an orphan, a farmer, and a preacher. Like the apostle Paul, he would never take a salary from the church, but farmed his land to support his family of ten. On Sundays and Wednesdays he was the pastor of the little white steepled church located in the center of the village.

The whole community knew him as "Uncle Sim" because of his kind and gentle spirit. Many stories were told of his "taking in" to his home those unfortunate, needy people who were the outcasts of society.

For sixty-three years he was "salt and light" in that community. His life was a testimony to all because of his integrity. Uncle Sim's "word was his bond."

The story of Simeon, in Luke's Gospel, reminded me so of my own grandpa that my inspiration turned into a poem about him. I was eleven at the time.

The passage from the Gospel of Luke reads:

"And behold, there was a man in Jerusalem whose name was Simeon, and this man was just and devout, waiting for the Consolation of Israel, and the Holy Spirit was upon him.

And it had been revealed to him by the Holy Spirit that he would not see death before he had seen the Lord's Christ.

So He came by the Spirit into the temple. And when the parents brought in the child Jesus, to do for Him according to the custom of the law, he took Him up in his arms and blessed God and said:

'Lord, now you are letting Your servant depart in peace, according to Your word; for my eyes have seen Your salvation which you have prepared before the face of all peoples,

A light to bring revelation to the Gentiles,

And the glory of Your people Israel.'

And Joseph and His mother marveled at those things which were spoken of Him

Then Simeon blessed them, and said to Mary His mother,

"Behold this Child is destined for the fall and rising of many in Israel, and for a sign which will be spoken against....(yes, a sword will pierce through your own soul also), that the thoughts of many hearts may be revealed."

LUKE 2:25-35 NKJ

MY GRANDPA

My grandpa's name is Simeon —
Reminds me of that one of old
Who was a just and devout man,
And in a message from God was told
That he should see the Christ-child
Before he passed away;
And in grandpa's experience
He sees the Savior today.
The Lord has dealt with my grandpa
In many a wondrous way;

Simeon Routh, Betty's Grandfather

In healing, sickness and sorrow,
But encouraging every day.
As he lay on a bed of sickness,
The Lord revealed his state,
Showing his past and future,
But this did not mean his fate.
For the Lord is good and forgiving
If we will wait, yielded and still;
Ready to do what He wants us
As we live in His Divine will.
As we journey the last mile of life's pathway,
The Lord seems so precious and near,
And as you trod onward rejoicing,
I know you'll make heaven, grandpa dear.

Betty Ruppert, age 11

GODLY FEAR — MY HERITAGE

I made my decision early. Though just a young girl of eleven, I was already thinking seriously when I knelt at the plain wooden altar in my grandpa's little country church Perhaps the circumstances in our family helped shape me to early maturity.

Even though my mother was a minister's daughter, she did not seriously follow the Lord until she was nearly 30. When she did, it seemed "all hell broke loose." My dad vigorously opposed her commitment to Christ.

Dad's drinking and gambling increased and he became physically abusive. He tried to "shake religion" out of my little sister, Patty, and threatened to kill the preacher with his loaded gun. Finally, after literally throwing mother into the street, he landed in jail for assault and battery.

Soon after that, our father deserted us and disappeared, leaving no clue for many years. So life became grim for a mother with two girls to support. She sub-leased our little rented cottage and the three of us moved into a small upstairs room in a nearby rooming house. We shared a bath at the end of a long hall with a number of other tenants on the same floor.

In our room there was a two-burner hot plate, a tiny table with two chairs and a lumpy bed. All three of us slept cross-wise on the bed with our feet hanging off, to give a little more sleeping space.

Mother bought a little feather-weight Singer sewing machine for $75. The payments were $3 per month and she took in sewing — mostly alterations for a men's clothing store. She never worked outside the home, feeling strongly the need to be close by for her girls.

Betty's mother, Birdie Rupp

We learned much about survival and God's provision!

Our meals were mostly potato soup, though from time to time we would find a bag of groceries outside our door. There was never a clue as to where they came from.

Without car or buses, we walked everywhere. Our clothes were given to us and we made them "over." That's where I learned to sew — no lessons, just desire. I wanted to be a dress designer.

My first job at age 11 was cleaning houses for fifty cents a day. My employer, a wise, kindly mentor, would liken me to Cinderella scrubbing the hearth, but also reminded me — that even Cinderella, one day, became a princess.

Since there was no money for a $3 activity ticket at school, joining the band was a way to attend the football games free. I could also have free music lessons, if I took whatever instrument was available, so the bassoon became my fatal assignment. God must have known I would need strong lungs and legs in life, so lugging that big case to school and church was part of my "basic training." I have said, "the next time around, I'll choose the piccolo — that, I can carry in my purse."

My love for music seemed thwarted because of no piano and no money for lessons. But mother found a way. After we moved from the rooming house, our home became a "free storage" for pianos, so we were never without one. A few lessons at a time, and with the use of my girlfriends' worn piano books, my heart's desire became reality. I spent many hours loving my music.

Our lives centered around the church, and we became a part of the family of God, that loved and taught the "whole Truth and nothing but the Truth." We were blest to have the strong teaching of the Scripture by pastors who were sound Bible teachers.

*Grandmother Ruppert & her Bible
with Vicki & Judi*

My mother's passion was to study the Word. She would read it aloud to me while I combed my hair before school. During the nearly fifty years she lived in our home, the daily sights and sounds were "mother studying her Bible by the front window" and prayers ascending from her basement room.

The role of the "intercessor" became her call and she never wavered in her claim of a "lamb for a house," Exodus 12:3, in the matter of my dad's salvation.

Her influence was felt far and wide through her letters, prayers and Bible studies. She was still teaching a Bible class at Calvary Temple in her 80's. Most of her prayers were for her family, friends, and the congregation where my husband pastored for more than fifty years.

No doubt it was her encouragement that prompted me to start teaching a class of "little tots" when I was still a teen-ager. Learning and teaching has continued to be a pattern of my life. It's not because I am a great communicator — I feel like Moses, most of the time — slow of speech, but rather when I teach, I'm sharing the greatest story of all time!

"How great is Thy goodness, which Thou hast stored up for those who fear Thee."

PSALM 31:19a

"AND HIS MERCY IS UPON GENERATION AFTER GENERATION TOWARDS THOSE WHO FEAR HIM."

LUKE 1:50

THE "REST OF THE STORY"

Both of my grandfathers were preachers. Both lived in the same little town in Kansas. Both had a small parish — one Methodist, the other Disciples of Christ. And both were present at the time of the historic "Holy Spirit outpouring" in the early 1900's in the region of Topeka, Kansas.

One believed and received the experience. The other rejected and ridiculed it.

One left a legacy of faith with his family of eight children and many more grandchildren actively serving God. (I've lost count of how many are in the ministry.)

The other saw his own life and family torn apart by adultery, divorce and alcohol.

My mother came from one — my father, the other.

* * * * * * *

When the call came, it was from the Printer's Union. They had been trying for days to locate a relative to claim the body of my dad, who had passed away in a Kaiser Hospital in San Francisco, California.

My husband and I flew there and gave him a funeral service and burial. We were the only persons attending. They presented us with a small box containing his earthly belongings and an insurance policy made out to his daughters for $1,000.

He died of cirrhosis of the liver — alone — without friends.

This very sad story is hopeful because of two things:

Just a few months prior to this, my mother took a rare shopping trip to downtown Denver all by herself; and whom should she run into — face-to-face on the street — but my dad. He came to our home for dinner and to meet the granddaughters he had never seen. We loved him and treated him with "open arms."

I visited his dingy hotel room and washed his socks, as he seemed very tired and shaky. He promised us that he would go back to San Francisco, get some things straightened out, and return to Denver.

When I put him on that Greyhound Bus and said "goodbye," I didn't know that I would never see him alive again.

We searched for any reassurance from nurses and staff about his last hours on earth, to know if he made "peace with God." We could find none.

But our hope and trust are in the fact that we, as a family, did not give up praying for and loving him — believing God to be faithful to His promise of "a lamb for a house."

In my own lifetime I have seen the sad, but dramatic portrayal of God's heart-cry:

> *"Oh, that they had such a heart in them, that they would fear Me and always keep all My commandments, that it might be well with them and with their children forever!"*
>
> DEUTERONOMY 5:29 NKJ

Simeon & Cora Routh and children
Birdie, Lillie, Lester, Eva, Nellie, Raymond & Lewis

For Every Fear
God has provided a
"FEAR NOT"

"For no temptation — no trial regarded as enticing to sin (no matter how it comes or where it leads) — has overtaken you and laid hold on you that is not common to man — that is,

no temptation or trial has come to you that is beyond human resistance and that is not adjusted and adapted and belonging to human experience, and such as man can bear.

But GOD IS FAITHFUL (to His Word and to His compassionate nature), and He (can be trusted) not to let you be tempted and tried and assayed beyond your ability and strength of resistance and power to endure,

but with the temptation He will (always) also provide the way out — the means of escape to a landing place — that you may be capable and strong and powerful patiently to bear up under it."

I CORINTHIANS 10:13 TAB

Part Two

Seven Natural Fears Of Life

Fear of:

Failure

Famine

Sickness

Danger

Suffering

Future

Death

"Fear Not, for I am with you;
Be not dismayed, for I am your God.
I will strengthen you, Yes, I will help you,
I will uphold you with My
righteous right hand."

Psalm 41:10

1
FAILURE

How could I ever forget that day?

The beautiful November day in Dallas ended in infamy and sent America reeling in shock and grief. Our young president, John Kennedy had been assassinated before thousands, as he rode in an open-car parade.

But I also remember it because it was the day they brought our firstborn, Vickie, home from school paralyzed. She was a senior in high school and had been involved in the SAT testing in preparation for college entrance.

Of course, she was hospitalized — then given a series of tests and diagnosed with a form of arthralgia, not organic in origin, but probably psychosomatic. The solution was to relieve all pressure possible and secure counseling.

It was soon after that I found myself on the floor by my bed crying out to God for Vickie's healing. The dialogue went something like this:

GOD: "What is it you want for Vickie?"

Betty: "Lord, you know what I most want. I'm her mother. I want the best — health, happiness, the good things in life."

GOD: "Don't you know that My love for her is greater than yours?"

Betty: "Oh, no, God! You don't understand — I'm her mother. You don't know what it's like to be a mother!"

GOD: "And where do you think that 'mother love' came from?"

I had to ponder that question for a while — and when I finally realized that my love was but an infinitesimal fraction of God's love — it was as if the windows of that room flung open wide and the sunlight came pouring in.

I could not doubt that God wanted to heal her. Of course, He did! He is more gracious and loving than the strongest mother's love.

Then my prayer changed from "God, heal her"...to:

"God, show me what it is You are wanting to teach us in this experience?"

> *Unbelief became impossible.*

He then encouraged me with that most heartening of verses from the Apostle Paul to Timothy:

> *"For God has not given us a spirit of fear, but of power and love and a sound mind."*
>
> II TIMOTHY 1:7

A few days later I found this note on my bed:

> *"The task ahead is never as great as the power behind."*

"I will go to college if you want me to, but you don't know what it's like to be afraid of everything."

Signed, Vickie

FEAR OF FAILURE — IT CAN IMMOBILIZE, EVEN PARALYSE.

The Lord did touch and heal Vickie and she did go to college!

FEAR OF FAILURE

Vickie

When we think of Moses, we remember him as the greatest of leaders-perhaps the most outstanding in Biblical history. But we forget just how inadequately he judged himself when God first called him.

> *"Then Moses said unto the Lord, 'Please, Lord, I have never been eloquent, neither recently nor in time past, nor since Thou hast spoken to Thy servant; for I am slow of speech and slow of tongue.'*

And the Lord said to him, 'Who has made man's mouth? Or who makes him dumb or deaf, or seeing or blind? Is it not I, the Lord?

Now then go, and I, even I, will be with your mouth, and teach you what you are to say.'

But he said, 'Please, Lord, now send the message by whomever Thou wilt.'"

EXODUS 4:10-13

I am also sure that Joshua had some moments of doubt and trepidation when he was handed the baton of leadership to follow Moses. He probably thought, "Am I to walk in the footsteps of that giant of wisdom and grace? No way!"

But God graciously reassured him with the promise:

"As I was with Moses, so I will be with thee."

JOSHUA 1:5

Joshua may not have had the *presence of mind,* as Moses, but he would have the *presence of God,* which is all he needed. To re-emphasize his divine call, three times God said: *"be strong and courageous!"*

"On that day the Lord exalted Joshua in the sight of all Israel; so that they revered him, just as they had revered Moses all the days of his life."

JOSHUA 4:14

There are several significant lessons we can learn from these passages. And probably most of us can identify with all of them.

First, these two great leaders were human beings just like you and me. And yet...God used them in spite of their weaknesses. Isn't that encouraging? That means there is hope for each of us. In spite of our shortcomings, our failures or our weaknesses, God can use us for His glory!

Second, Moses needed to arrive at a balance in his life between *"self-confidence"* and *"God-confidence."* He went to two extremes. First he said, "I can't do it!" Then he said, "I can do it!"

For the Christian, both are true when stated properly.   Paul said,

"I can do all things through Him who strengthens me"

PHILIPPIANS 4:13

Third, and perhaps most important, Moses failed to see what God was attempting to accomplish in his life, in spite of his personal failure. God took a bad experience, one of Moses' own making, and used it to equip him for his future ministry.

You see, God knew what lay ahead for Moses. He knew that Moses' rejection in Egypt 40 years before would fade into nothingness in relationship to the rejection he would face in the future as he began carrying out God's will and led the children of Israel out of bondage. The *very thing* that caused Moses to almost miss God's will actually *enabled him* to handle the even greater problems that lay ahead.

All of us face problems that we do not understand. It is not right to blame God for structuring these circumstances, for they are frequently caused by the sins of others. At other times they are of our own doing. The important point is that God can take a bad experience, no matter who caused it, and turn it into *a blessing* — that is, if we see things from God's perspective.

And what is God's perspective? Paul stated it succinctly:

"And we know that God causes all things to work together for good to those who love God, to those who are called according to His purpose."

ROMANS 8:28

God is pleased sometimes to make a choice of those as His messengers who have fewest of the advantages of art or nature, that His grace in them may appear all the more glorious. Christ's disciples were no orators, 'till the Spirit made them such.

"Courage comes from the continual consciousness of the presence of Christ."

FEAR NOTS FOR FAILURE-

"For I know the plans I have for you, declares the Lord. They are plans for good and not for evil, to give you a future and a hope."

JEREMIAH 29:11 TLB

"For Thou didst form my inward parts; Thou didst weave me in my mother's womb. I will give thanks to Thee, for I am fearfully and wonderfully made; wonderful are Thy works, and my soul knows it very well. My frame was not hidden from Thee, when I was made in secret, and skillfully wrought in the depths of the earth. Thine eyes have seen my unformed substance; and in Thy book they were all written, The days that were ordained for me, When as yet there was not one of them."

PSALMS 139:13-16

> *Courage is fear that has prayed.*

*"But the very hairs of your head are all numbered. Therefore **do not fear;** you are of more value than many sparrows."*

MATTHEW 10:30

*"Know that the Lord Himself is God; It is **He who has made us**, and not we ourselves; We are his people and the sheep of his pasture."*

PSALMS 100:3

"There once was a man
Who never took a risk in life,
   Then, at the last
His insurance was denied;
   So they said —
That since he never really lived,
   Then — he never really died!"
          Anonymous

Vickie, Charles, Betty & Judi

*"For thus says the
Lord God of Israel: 'The bin of flour
shall not be used up, nor shall the
jar of oil run dry.....*"*

1 Kings 17:14

2
FAMINE
(Finances)

An interview with a knowledgeable financial advisor on nationwide television was one that painted a rather dismal picture. Here's what he said:

1. Exports will go down.

2. Capitol spending will go down.

3. Consumer spending (which is 68% of the economy) will go down.

4. Government spending is going up.

He added: "We are probably facing the greatest and longest slowdown in a decade. The world is facing eruptions everywhere. We are in a very uneasy, uncertain and nervous position."

From the Wall Street Journal, October 19, 2001:

....UPS net slid 19%....expressed little hope of a turnaround in time for its crucial year- end shipping season.

....ALLSTATE reported a 65% decline in 3rd quarter net on deeper losses from its homeowners insurance business.

....RAYTHEON posted a loss and slashed forecasts for this year and next, due to falling demand for its commercial planes.

....BELLSOUTH said it will lay off 3,000 workers, as the phone company reported that quarterly net income plunged 99%.

….MERRILL LYNCH'S earnings fell over 50% amid a sharp decline in brokerage business and further deterioration following the September 11 terrorist attacks.

….COMPUTER ASSOCIATES reported a net loss of 291 million for its fiscal 2nd quarter on a 52% decline in revenue.

The "famine" of 2001 may not resemble that of Old Testament times, but it may do every bit as much damage. It is noteworthy that famine was one of the things God used to punish sin and disobedience. Leviticus 26:26; Deuteronomy 28:53; Jeremiah 14:16

We also see it listed as one of the signs of the second coming of Christ in Matthew 24.

The 1980 Economy was in serious slump — worldwide.

Following is a statement made by a gentleman from Belgium by the name of Paul Andre' Spock. Mr. Spock was one of the organizational leaders of the "Society for World-Wide Inter-Bank Financial Tele-Communications" and his comments were made in a speech to the United European Community. In speaking to this distinguished group of leaders, he said:

"What we want is a man of sufficient stature to hold the allegiance of all people — to lift us out of the economic morass in which we are sinking. Send us such a man — whether he be God or devil, we'll accept him!"

There are many instances of famine recorded in the Scripture. Just to name a few:

*"And there were others who said: 'We are mortgaging our fields, our vineyards, and our houses that we might get grain because of the **famine.**'"*
                                                                    NEHEMIAH 5:3

*"On the ninth day of the fourth month the **famine** was so severe in the city that there was no food for the people of the land."*
                                                                    II KINGS 25:3

*"And there was a great **famine** in Samaria; and behold, they besieged it, until a donkey's head was sold for 80 shekels of silver, and a fourth of a kab of dove's dung for five shekels of silver."*

II KINGS 6:25

*"Now there was a **famine** in the land; so Abram went down to Egypt to sojourn there, for the **famine** was severe in the land."*

GENESIS 12:10

*"…then there was famine in all the lands; but in all the land of Egypt there was bread. When the famine was spread over all the face of the earth, then Joseph opened all the storehouses, and sold to the Egyptians; and the **famine** was severe in the land of Egypt."*

GENESIS 41:54, 56

We read of it also in:

the days of the judges: Ruth 1:1
the reign of Ahab: I Kings17:1; 18:5
time of Elisha: II Kings 4:38
and Jeremiah: Jeremiah14:1

WAR

It was often accompanied by war: Jeremiah 14:15; 29:17, 18

PESTILENCE

And followed by pestilence: Jeremiah 42:17; Ezekial 7:15

SIN

More than once, it was on account of sin

*If then, you act with hostility against Me, and are unwilling to obey Me, I will increase the **plague** on you seven times according to your sins."*

LEVITICUS 26:21

*"….you will eat and **not be satisfied**."*

LEVITICUS 26:26

"Now there was a **famine** in the days of David for 3 years, year, after year; and David sought the presence of the Lord.

And the Lord said: 'It is for Saul and his bloody house, because he put the Gibeonites to death.'"

II SAMUEL 21:1

"The tongue of the infant cleaves to the roof of its mouth because of **thirst;** the little ones **ask for bread,** but no one breaks it for them. Those who ate delicacies are desolate in the streets; those reared in purple embrace ash pits.

For the iniquity of the daughter of my people is greater than the sin of Sodom, which was overthrown as in a moment, and no hands were turned toward her."

LAMENTATIONS 4:4-6

"…the ground is cracked, for there has been no rain on the land…even the doe in the field has given birth only to abandon her young, because there is no grass.

Thus says the Lord to this people: 'Even so they have loved to wander; they have not kept their feet in check. Therefore the Lord does not accept them; now He will remember their iniquity and call their sins to account.'

So the Lord said to me, 'Do not pray for the welfare of this people. When they fast, I am not going to listen to their cry; and when they offer burnt offerings, I am not going to accept them. Rather, I am going to make an end of them by the sword, **famine** and pestilence.'"

JEREMIAH 14:4,5, 10-12

JUDGEMENT

We see it over and over again-that *famine* was one of God's four sore judgments;

"For thus says the Lord God, 'How much more when I send My four severe judgments against Jerusalem; sword, **famine**, wild beasts, and plague to cut off man and beast from it!"

EZEKIEL 14:21

But we find a most remarkable story of God's ability to supercede circumstances and provide for His own in Genesis 26: 1-5 and 12-14:

> "*Now there was **a famine** in the land, besides the previous **famine** that had occurred in the days of Abraham. So Isaac went to Gerar, to Abimelech the king of the Philistines.*
>
> *And the Lord appeared to him and said, 'Do not go down to Egypt; stay in the land of which I shall tell you. Sojourn in this land and I will be with you and bless you, for to you and to your descendants I will give all these lands, and I will establish the oath which I swore to your father Abraham.*
>
> *And I will multiply your descendants as the stars of heaven, and will give your descendants all these lands; and by your descendants all the nations of the earth shall be blessed; because Abraham obeyed Me and kept My charge, My commandments, My statutes and My laws.' So Isaac lived in Gerar...*
>
> *Now Isaac sowed in that land, and **reaped in the same year a hundredfold. And the Lord blessed him.***
>
> *And the man became rich, and continued to grow richer until he became very wealthy; for he had possessions of flocks and herds and a great household, so that the Philistines envied him.*"

Famine will bring you no fear.

GOD KEPT HIS PROMISE!

He took care of His own! And more than that — right in the midst of *famine* God so blessed that Isaac reaped a hundredfold in the same year.

MY TEST

In the midst of one of the major trials of our life, which included a lawsuit and a court trial, the Lord put me to the test in the area of finances.

My husband just casually said, as he passed through the kitchen: "Would it be O.K. to give our $30,000 in the offering tomorrow?" This was a note owed to us personally by the church. In reality, it was the equity in our home.

In the pit of my stomach, I felt sick.

I was trying to rebound. I wasn't ready for surprises of this sort.

Thoughts were racing through my head too fast to decipher:

"That's 25 years of house payments."

"That's all the security I really have!"

"Who will take care of me when I get old?"

I felt shaky…I had to go pray. "Lord, help me!"

Sunday morning found us in our usual places: me at the console of the Allen organ; my husband, the pastor, at the large mahogany pulpit on the platform...

Then I heard that most familiar voice exclaim to the congregation: "Rejoice with me," he was saying, "someone has just given $30,000 for the fund drive!"

A little bit stunned, I was thinking: "I can't believe he's really doing this." Actually, I was hoping for a last minute reprieve.

Then I heard: "Betty, would you come, take a paper brick off the wall, and bring it to me?"

My heart was pounding — my mind was wavering — my emotions were teetering — I wanted to take the next "slow boat to China." Instead, I took the longest route possible via the hallway, finally making it to the platform, brick in hand.

Then, his voice: "My dear, would you pray over this?"

Needless to say, the dam burst. I couldn't pray — all I could do was cry. For in that moment, my emotions engulfed me.

After the service, our son-in-law exclaimed:

"Isn't it wonderful, someone gave $30,000?"

I was thinking: "Boy, you'll think it's wonderful when you have to take care of me when I'm old!"

The next day I was still struggling; but in a time of prayer the Lord gave to me Mark 10: 28-30:

"Peter began to say to Him, 'Behold, we have left everything and followed You.' Jesus said: 'Truly I say to you, there is no one who has left house or brothers or sisters or mothers or fathers or children or farms, for My sake and for the gospel's sake, but that he shall receive a hundred times as much now in the present age, houses and brothers, and sisters, and mothers and children and farms, along with persecutions; and in the world to come, eternal life."

With that promise God gave an enormous flood of joy and peace. I never gave it a moment's thought again. In fact, I almost get giddy when I think: "Jesus is going to take care of me when I get old!"

God gave me another tremendous promise from Hebrews 13: 5, 6: NIV

"Keep your lives free from the lust for money; be content with what you have, for He Himself has said: 'I will never leave you nor forsake you, so that we may boldly say, The Lord is my Helper and I will not fear what man shall do unto me.'"

I especially love the Amplified Version of that passage:

"He (God) Himself has said, 'I will not in any way fail you nor give you up nor leave you without support. **I will not, I will not, I will not**, *in any degree leave you helpless, nor forsake nor let you down (relax My hold on you) — Assuredly not!'"*

Did you notice the triple negative!

"So we take comfort and are encouraged and confidently and boldly say, 'The Lord is my Helper, I will not be seized with alarm — I will not fear or dread or be terrified, What can man do to me?"

PSALMS. 118: 6 AND 27:1

In the trial of *famine* and *finances*, we need often to review and repeat to ourselves the promises we have been given, especially when we recognize that our faith is being tested.

"HE IS NO FOOL WHO GIVES WHAT HE CANNOT KEEP TO GAIN WHAT HE CANNOT LOSE."

JIM ELLIOT, MARTYR TO THE AUCAS.

GOD'S PROSPERITY

Paul gives to us a marvelous truth in his writings to the Phillipians when he thanks them for attending to his material needs:

"But I rejoiced in the Lord greatly that now at last your care for me has flourished again; though you surely did care, but you lacked opportunity.

Not that I speak in regard to need, for I have learned in whatever state I am, to be content: I know how to be abased, and I know how to abound.

Everywhere and in all things I have learned both to be full and to be hungry, both to abound and to suffer need. I can do all things through Christ who strengthens me."

PHILIPPIANS 4:10-13 NKJ

Here is a guiding light to understanding God's will on the subject of prosperity. It tells us *yes* (we can have riches), and *no* (do not trust in them.) Here is assurance that if our lives are geared to the Word of God, then, through Christ, we can experience either wealth or temporary setback, but we will still be steadfast in our living, all because our trust will be only in Him.

If the economy should dissolve tomorrow, God's people would not be rendered inoperative, because *God is our source.* He can keep us through times of scarcity as well as in times of plenty.

If God could nourish Corrie ten Boom in the confines of a Nazi concentration camp, (the vitamin bottle never ran out); if He could furnish a table in the wilderness, make ravens to be purveyors, cooks and servers to a prophet, then He is able to supply our needs as well. He is the same today as He was then. He will be our Jehovah-Jireh!

FEAR NOTS FOR FAMINE

*"And it shall be that you shall drink of the brook, and I have commanded the **ravens to provide** for you there."*

"And the ravens brought him bread and meat in the morning and bread and meat in the evening, and he would drink from the brook."

I KINGS 17:4, 6

*" Do not fear...make me a little cake first...so she went and did...she and her house ate for many days. The bowl of flour **was not exhausted** nor did the jar of oil become empty, according to the word of the Lord..."*

I KINGS 17:13-16

*"They shall not be ashamed in the evil time, and in the days of **famine** they shall be satisfied."*

PSALMS 37:19 NKJ

*"Do not be anxious for your life, as to what you shall eat, or what you shall drink; nor for your body, as to what you shall put on. Is not life more than food, and the body than clothing? Look at the birds of the air, they do not sow, neither do they reap, nor gather into barns and yet **your heavenly Father feeds them**. Are you not worth much more than they?"*

MATTHEW 6:25, 26

"Peace
I leave with you:
not as the world gives
do I give to you.
Let not your heart be troubled,
neither
let it be afraid."

John 14:27 NKJ

3
SICKNESS

FEAR IS COSTLY

Doctors agree: Fears are the most disruptive thing we can have. For example — the incidence of stomach ulcers goes up and down with the stock market. Investigation showed that when the Dow-Jones averages on the stock market skidded down, the number of businessmen with upset stomachs went up. Worry would bring an over-acidity of stomach, and that in turn would upset the digestive tract.

Men of old saw the connection between worry and disease: *"Banish all worries from your mind and keep your body free from pain."* Ecclesiastes 11:10 Moffatt

Since September 11 there does not seem to be so much concern about cholesterol and cancer as much as the new threats of bio-chemical warfare. Every new headline seems geared to fear.

A news release from Fox network tells of the 7 most-likely diseases to be unleashed in a bio-chemical attack on America. Among them:

A modern day "black plague" similar to the deadly Bubonic plague, only this one is a "pneumonic plague." It comes from the root word, "pestilence."

Smallpox which was thought to have been eradicated, since there have been no cases since 1949. We are now told that we have an "unvaccinated" generation and even those who were vaccinated, may no longer be immune.

Bebola, a deadly African virus has an 80% death rate and no known cure!

And then there is SARS (severe acute respiratory syndrome,) the mysterious and highly contagious illness, surfacing in new unexpected places,

69

with a whole load of unknowns. As of May, 2003, more than 7200 persons had been infected in more than 25 countries, boosting the death count to at least 526. China alone has reported more than 4,800 SARS cases. Human beings wearing surgical masks and eye goggles became a familiar sight in some parts of the world.

– Associated Press, May, 2003

This kind of information should not panic us, and yet we are not immune to fear. We still open our mail, but now with more thoughtfulness.

Before Adam sinned no infirmity of any kind existed; sickness arose only after the fall.

Had man not fallen, sickness would not have come upon the earth. Hence, as with every other woe, sickness was ushered in by sin. It is the nemesis of man and it is used as a tool of Satan. Job 2:7

God also used *sickness* as a vehicle, both constructively and destructively, to demonstrate His Almighty power over the powers of darkness.

From the early pages of the Bible, we read how God *protected His people*, Israel, from the plagues and diseases that came upon the other nations around them. It appears that *"the eyes of the Lord run to and fro throughout the whole earth,"* and through the air too, to serve some great and designed end, that he may show Himself strong on the behalf of those whose hearts are upright. II Chronicles 16:9

SPECIAL IMMUNITY

*"But on that day I will **set apart** the land of Goshen, where my people are living, so that no swarms of insects will be there, in order that you may know that I, the Lord, am in the midst of the land. And I will **put a division** between My people and your people. Tomorrow this sign shall occur."*

EXODUS 8:22, 23

*"So the Lord did this thing on the morrow, and all the livestock of Egypt died; but of the livestock of the sons of Israel, **not one died.**"*

EXODUS 9:6

*"So Moses stretched out his hand toward the sky, and there was thick darkness in all the land of Egypt for three days. They did not see one another, nor did anyone rise from his place for three days, but all the **sons of Israel had light in their dwellings.**"*

EXODUS 10: 22, 23

*"Moreover, there shall be a great cry in all the land of Egypt, such as there has not been before and such as shall never be again. But against any of the sons of Israel a dog shall not even bark, whether against man or beast, that you may understand how the **Lord makes a distinction between Egypt and Israel.**"*

EXODUS 11:6, 7

*"And the blood shall be a sign to you on the houses where you live; and when I see the blood I will pass over you, and **no plague will befall you** to destroy you when I strike the land of Egypt."*

EXODUS 12:13

"Then those who feared the Lord spoke to one another, and the Lord gave attention and heard it, and a book of remembrance was written before Him for those who fear the Lord and who esteem His name.

*'And they will be Mine,' says the Lord of hosts, 'on the day that I prepare My own possession, and **I will spare them** as a man spares his own son who serves him.'*

*So you will again **distinguish between the righteous and the wicked,** between one who serves God and one who does not serve Him."*

MALACHI 3:16-18

WHY HE CHOSE ISRAEL

BLESSINGS ON OBEDIENCE

I am always overwhelmed by the magnanimous heart of God when I read:

*"The Lord did not set His love on you nor choose you because you were more in number than any of the peoples, for you were the fewest of all peoples, but **because the Lord loved you** and kept the oath which He swore to your forefathers, the Lord brought you out by a mighty hand and redeemed you from the house of slavery, from the hand of Pharaoh king of Egypt."*

DEUTERONOMY 7:7, 8

TWENTY ONE BLESSINGS
Deuteronomy 28: 1-14

1. God will *set you on high* above all other nations of the earth and all these blessings shall come upon you and overtake you. vs. 1, 2

2. You will be blessed in the city. vs. 3

3. You will be blessed in the field. vs. 3

4. You will have perfect offspring. vs. 4

5. Your crops will be blessed. vs.4

6. Your flocks will increase. vs.4

7. Your cattle will increase. vs.4

8. Your basket and storehouses will be full. vs. 5, 8

9. You will be blessed in all you undertake. vs. 6

10. Complete victory over all your enemies. vs. 7

11. Land will be abundantly fertile and productive. vs.8

12. Establish as a holy people to God. vs. 9

13. A witness and example to all people on earth. vs. 10

14. All nations will be afraid of you. vs.10

15. Prosperous in goods, children, stock, crops. vs. 11

16. The Lord will open all His good treasure. vs. 12

17. Heavens will give you rain in due season. vs.12

18. Lord will bless all the work of your hands. v.8

19. Will be prosperous enough to lend to many nations, and you will not need to borrow from them. vs.12

20. Lord will make you the head, not the tail. vs.13

21. You shall be above all men and never beneath them. vs. 13

FIVE CONDITIONS
Deuteronomy 28:1-14

1. If you hearken diligently to the voice of the Lord. vs. 1-2, 9, 13, 15

2. If you observe and do all His commandments. vs. 1, 13, 15

3. If you walk in His ways. vs. 9

4. If you do not go aside from any of the words of God, to the right hand or left. vs. 13, 14

5. If you do not go after other gods to serve them. vs. 14

FEAR NOTS FOR SICKNESS:

*"If you will give earnest heed to the voice of the Lord your God, and do what is right in His sight, and give ear to His commandments, and keep all His statutes, **I will put none of the diseases** on you which I have put on the Egyptians; for **I, the Lord, am your healer.**"*

EXODUS 15:26

*But you shall serve the Lord your God, and He will **bless your bread and your water**; and I **will remove sickness** from your midst."*

EXODUS 23:25

"And He will love you and bless you and multiply you; He will also bless the fruit of your womb and the fruit of your ground, your grain and your new wine and your oil, the increase of your herd and the young of your flock, in the land which He swore to your forefathers to give you.

You shall be blessed above all peoples; there shall be no male or female barren among you or among your cattle.

*And the Lord will **remove from you all sickness**, and He will not put on you any of the harmful diseases of Egypt which you have known, but He will lay them on all who hate you."*

DEUTERONOMY 7:13-15

HEALTH PROMISED

*"My son, give attention to my words; incline your ear to my sayings. Do not let them depart from your sight; keep them in the midst of your heart, for they are **life** to those who find them, and **health** to all their whole body."*

PROVERBS 4:20, 22

*"For I will restore you to **health** and I will **heal** you of your wounds, declares the Lord."*

JEREMIAH 30:17

*"Those who wait for the Lord will gain **new strength**…"*

ISAIAH 40:31

*"He was wounded for our transgressions, He was bruised for our iniquities; the chastisement for our peace was upon Him, and by His stripes we are **healed**."*

ISAIAH 53:5 NKJ

*"**Heal** the sick, raise the dead, cleanse the lepers, cast out demons; freely you received, freely give."*

MATTHEW 10:8

MY PRESCRIPTION

In the midst of our "crisis," I paid my annual visit to my gynecologist, who was a very fine Jewish doctor. During the visit, he asked the question:

"I know you must be under tremendous pressure — I do read the newspapers. Are you taking any medication?"

"No, nothing." I answered, "not even aspirin."

"Would you like something?" he asked; but it was more than a question, as he wrote out a prescription.

I thanked him — and on arriving home, I tucked the new prescription away in my jewelry box.

About a year later I noticed the little white slip in the same place, still unfilled. At the time I just happened to be reading two great classics: *The Pursuit of God,* by A. W. Tozer and *The Normal Christian Life* by Watchman Nee. Then I realized, "Here is my real prescription!"

Sometime later, a mutual friend told me of the doctor's comments about the Blairs:

"That must be some God they have!"

It's true! And — the most powerful prescription in the world is God's Word!

John 6:63: *"It is the Spirit who gives life; the flesh profits nothing; the words that I have spoken to you are **spirit** and are **life.**"*

" *God's blessing*
makes life rich;
nothing we do
can improve on God. "
Proverbs 10:22 MSG

Early Days

*Parents Virgil & Birdie Ruppert,
Patty and Betty*

Charles & Betty, young Evangelists

1st date with Charles

*1st Family, 1st Church
Betty, Judi, Vickie & Mother Ruppert*

Calvary Temple Days

Pastors, Calvary Temple 51 years

Calvary Temple Congregation

Calvary Temple Days
Betty's Ministry

Betty's "Day Spring" Bible Study

Love that tamborine!

"Day Spring Luncheon"
Blair & Morgan with mother, Bobbie

Betty at the Allen Organ

Celebration Days
25 yrs!

*Red Rocks Celebration, 25 years as pastor
Hale & Wilder, guest soloists*

*"Well done!" 40th Anniversary Celebration
as pastor of Calvary Temple*

*Ron & Donna Huff, Music
Directors and Betty &
Charles, at Red Rocks*

*25th Anniversary Celebration as Pastors of Calvary Temple,
Red Rocks Amphitheater, Denver, Co.*

Calvary Temple Friends

Betty – Corrie ten Boom – Charles
At Calvary Temple, Denver

Missions at Calvary Temple with Bob Pierce,
founder of World Vision

Friends and Authors, John & Elizabeth Sherrill

Around The World In 80 days
(Almost)

Touring the Greek Islands with pilots, Mike & Gail Allen

Bedoin's tent - Shepherd's Field - Israel

Temple Mount, Israel

*Pastor Blair visiting
David Ben-Gurion
1st Prime Minister of Israel*

*Shepherd's
Fields, Israel*

Around The World Again . . .

Betty viewing Temple in China

In India visiting Mother Teresa with Ted Engstrom of World Vision

Taj Mahal, Agra, India

The Egyptian Taxi

and Again...

R & R with Charles E

Betty & Granddaughter Monica, in Alaska

Big game hunting in Africa

Marrles, Charles, Kodiak, Alaska

The one that didn't get away!

Charles, Marrles & Brian in Alaska

Mission Days

For more than a decade Charles Blair has been involved in mission work in Ethiopia. Working in concert with Evangelical Churches Fellowship of Ethiopia, he has assisted in the planting of more than 800 churches, as well as the training of at least 1,000 Ethiopian leaders and missionaries. There have been more than 50,000 newly baptized converts.

"Crown Prince Charles"
Awards and Rewards in
Ethiopia

Charles with Ethiopian children

"You will not be afraid of the terror
by night, Or of the arrow that flies by day;
Of the pestilence that stalks in darkness,
Or of the destruction that
lays waste at noon."

Psalm 91:5, 6

4
DANGER

"Any soldier who says he's not afraid, is a liar."

These words were spoken by Sen. John McCain in a wartime T.V. interview on LARRY KING LIVE. They were in response to the question:

"What's it like for a soldier going into battle?"

McCain replied with the authority of a veteran, for he was a Prisoner of War in Vietnam for five years. Mr. McCain knew first-hand some of the horrors of war. That's when he gave the famous quote: "No one hates war more than a warrior!"

David, however, of Bible times, seemed to contradict this axiom since he was a warrior of warriors. From the boyhood feat of taking out the giant, Goliath, with only a sling, to the many conquests as leader and king of Israel, David was known by this refrain:

> *"Saul has slain his thousands,*
> *But David his ten thousands."*

Perhaps it was because the Lord fought his battles for him!

But he also knew what it was to be a fugitive from Saul, hiding in the caves and strongholds of Engedi.

How strange it has been to hear and see in the news -

CAVES, ROCKS, HIDING PLACES, SHIELD, DEFENSE...

These words are suddenly a part of our vocabulary as we fight the first war of the 21st century.

87

In our effort to "smoke out the enemy," we find ourselves using the language of the Bible.

It seems surreal…to go from computers to caves in the same sentence! It makes the writings of the psalmist more fitting, especially in the face of danger.

GOD IS OUR ROCK

"*For in the time of trouble He shall hide me in His pavilion; in the secret of His tabernacle shall He hide me; He shall set me high upon a **rock.***"

PSALMS 27:5 NKJ

"*For Thou art my **rock** and my fortress; therefore for Thy name's sake, lead me, and guide me.*"

PSALMS 31:3 KJ

"*From the end of the earth will I cry unto Thee, when my heart is overwhelmed: lead me to the **rock** that is higher than I.*"

PSALMS 61:2 KJ

"*But the Lord is my defense; and my God is the **rock** of my refuge.*"

PSALMS 94:22 KJ

REFUGE

"*The Lord also will be a refuge for the oppressed, **a refuge** in times of trouble.*"

PSALMS 9:9 KJ

"*God is our **refuge** and strength, a very present help in trouble.*"

PSALMS 46:1 KJ

"*Be merciful unto me, O God, be merciful unto me: for my soul trusteth in thee: yea, in the shadow of thy wings will make my **refuge,** until these calamities be over past.*"

PSALMS 57:1 KJ

"*In God is my salvation and my glory: the rock of my strength, and my **refuge,** is in God.*"

PSALMS 62:7 KJ

*"I will say of the Lord, He is my **refuge** and my fortress: my God; in him will I trust."*

PSALMS 91:2 KJ

*"I will sing of thy power; yea, I will sing aloud of thy mercy in the morning: for thou has been my defense and **refuge** in the day of my trouble."*

PSALMS 59:16 KJ

HIDING PLACE

*"Thou art my **hiding place**; thou shalt preserve me from trouble; thou shalt compass me about with songs of deliverance."*

PSALMS 32:7 KJ

*"**Hide** me from the secret counsel of evildoers, from the tumult of those who do iniquity."*

PSALMS 64:2

*"Thou art my **hiding place** and my shield;. I hope in thy word."*

PSALMS 119:114 KJ

*"Deliver me, O Lord, from mine enemies: I flee unto thee to **hide** me."*

PSALMS 143:9 KJ

SHIELD

*"The Lord is my strength and my **shield**; my heart trusts in Him and I am helped. Therefore my heart exults, and with my song I shall thank Him."*

PSALMS 28:7

*"For the Lord God is a sun and **shield**; the Lord gives grace and glory; no good thing does he withhold from those who walk uprightly."*

PSALMS 84:11

*"He shall cover thee with His feathers, and under His wings shalt thou trust: His truth shall be your **shield** and buckler."*

PSALMS 91:4 NKJ

MY SONG

I sing a lot — not always out loud, but in my mind and heart. It goes on day and night. Much of the time whatever my thoughts, they turn into phrases of a song or songs.

One of my favorites is ON EAGLE'S WINGS by Michael Joncas;

And one of the verses sings:

> "*The snare of the fowler will never capture you;*
> *And famine will bring you no fear,*
> *Under His wings, your refuge,*
> *His faithfulness, your shield.*" [1]

How can — I pondered, "*His faithfulness…*be *my shield?*" But as I thought upon it, I began to understand. In my mind I recounted the many times God has been there...not one time has He failed me; and my faith would rise with the memory of each experience; then, as a result, I felt strengthened to trust Him more! And that inner strength became a shield, protecting me from the darts of doubt that Satan would hurl at me. It's not something magic...and yet it is! It's a proven principle and it works!

BIG FEARS — LITTLE FEARS

I married a man who dreams big — a man whose imagination knows no bounds and whose energy is unsurpassed. Add to that a huge dose of persistence and self- discipline, plus a dash of stubbornness, and you have the ingredients for unlimited success or a whopping failure or two. And for his wife, it sometimes presents a problem. There can be a clash of philosophies, goals, priorities — and even ideas about what constitutes a vacation.

He loves adventure — from hunting polar bear in the Artic to stalking leopards and lions in Africa. He's done it all. The more risky — the more exhilarating!

And of course there are the endless trips around the country and around the world to preach and teach. But…he doesn't want to go alone. I think a part of his happiness is for me to tag along and watch him in action, cheering him on to the homeward stretch!

On the other hand, it is pure joy for me to "sink into" a good book in front of an open fire or spend a few quiet hours at the keyboard. So it seems much of my life has been decisions — whether to go or stay — his will or mine. And since he is the greatest of salesmen I'm usually left in a quandary of what to do.

Some of his arguments:

"You can shop." ("I can shop at home.")

"You can sleep." ("I can sleep at home.")

"You can be with me." ("You're in meetings much of the time.")

So I struggle with not wanting to "*go*" and not wanting to say, "*no.*" And some of these involve my own inner fears — seeing all the potential dangers, first.

There was the planned tour to Israel and the debate about canceling due to the violence and disruption in the Middle East. Of course, these things do not bother my husband — he is the eternal optimist!

I asked myself the questions:

"What is my responsibility here?"
"Whom will I disappoint?"
"Whom will I bless?"
"Do I go by my feelings?"

As I sought the Lord in the matter, I received my answer:

I will go in the name of the Lord and trust HIM to provide the grace and strength.

And, to my amazement—I did! And HE DID!

More recently, it was whether to join the grandkids for a rough-riding rafting trip down the Colorado river. Again, I thought of the dangers first; weighing the options and asking those intrusive questions.

No one expected me to join the party, but I surprised them. In fact, I surprised myself! But I discovered that when you forget about yourself and think of others, somehow *fear flees!*

Fear can manifest itself in a lot of different ways and under almost any circumstance. I've had some pretty rough rides over the Pacific, with the plane lurching and tossing like a rubber ball; but I find consolation in the words of David: "*What time I am afraid, I will trust in Thee.*" Psalms 56:3

Several times while pastoring the church in Denver the alarms sounded and our own lives were threatened. I can tell you this, at the time the drama was unfolding it was very real and very frightening!

Right in the middle of a Sunday evening service, a call was received concerning a bomb threat. We were advised to take the call seriously, so the whole congregation was evacuated and ended up singing outside on the church lawn while the building was searched by sniffing dogs – as well as the pastor's car in the parking lot.

Another evening about service time we started to enter the street bordering our parking lot when we were stopped by a barricade and police telling us we could not enter.

"We're under siege!" they shouted, waving us on.

"But, I'm the pastor of this church," my husband replied.

"Are you Blair?" they challenged, skeptically.

"Yes, I am and have been for most of my life," he said.

"Well, there's a gunman in there and he's holding a pastor hostage, and how many more we don't know." We thought you were the hostage being held.

Quickly, they shoved my husband into a squad car and whisked him across the parking lot to the back of the building, while I was told to huddle down on floor of our car and stay put until further instructions.

For the next two hours, we waited while the SWAT team, guided by the police and pastor, searched the many rooms, offices and closets of that huge building before finally giving us the "all clear" signal to enter.

These kinds of experiences always give a rush of adrenalin. But the verse I *cling* and *look to* in those dangerous moments is Isaiah 54:17:

"No weapon that is formed against you shall prosper;
And every tongue that accuses you in judgment you will condemn.
This is the heritage of the servants of the Lord,
And their vindication is from Me, declares the Lord."

Corrie ten Boom's sister, Betsie, said:

"There are no 'ifs' in God's world. And no places are safer than other places. The center of His will is our only safety — O Corrie, let us pray that we may always know it."

Fear is in the emotions; Faith is in the spirit.

THE SECRET PLACE

We learn from the Scripture that it *is possible* to live in regal serenity, free of fear, stable like a rock, with quiet assurance, even in the face of danger.

It is described in Psalm 91:

"He that dwelleth in the secret place of the Most High shall abide under the shadow of the Almighty."

In truth it means: Those who live in communion with God are constantly safe under His protection for He *"gives angels charge,"* He is our *"hiding place,"* He makes us to lie down in *"green pastures,"* and leads us beside *"still waters,"* He sets before us *"tables in the wilderness,"* and *"shelters"* us so that we experience peace in every situation, whether storm or sunshine.

What a promise! It gives to one security, serenity, peace, joy!

So, we immediately ask the question:

> What is this secret place?
> Where is it?
> Why is it secret?
> How can I find it? Can I live there?
> Is it even possible?

First of all, it is "secret" because it is a place not known, *except to the godly.*

It is a place because it is there that believers cannot be found and molested by the evil one.

God said to Moses:

"*There is a place by Me...*" Exodus 33:21

There is a place near to the heart of God..."*a place where sin cannot molest.*" It is that inner citadel of ourselves. That's where God wants to meet us.

The reason many of our prayers are empty and ineffective; they seldom come from the *secret* place. We are afraid to open the door of that inner citadel to God or ourselves. But when we do, we will discover a whole new world of *inner strength.*

We ask the question: "How can I find that *secret* place?

Is it possible to live there?"

THERE ARE TWO KEYS:

MEDITATION and SOLITUDE

"*...Meditate in your heart upon your bed, and be still.*"
PSALMS 4:4

"*I will remember my song in the night; I will meditate with my heart; and my spirit ponders.*"
PSALMS 77:6

"*My meditation of Him shall be sweet: I will be glad in the Lord.'*
PSALMS 104:34 KJ

"*Be still, and know that I am God.*"
PSALMS 46:10 KJ

To hear God's voice, turn down the world's volume.'

In our culture today the enemy of our soul majors in noise, hurry and crowds. But God requires time, "*alone time,*" in order to speak to us and reinforce our inner being with supernatural strength.

I love the way E. Stanley Jones puts it:

"In the pure, strong hours of the morning, when the soul of the day is its best, lean upon the windowsill of the Lord — look into His face — and get your orders for the day. Then go out into the world with a sense of *a Hand* on your shoulder and not a chip."

As we seek the Lord and meditate on His attributes, His character, His ways, His promises, we will find ourselves entering that "*secret place*" and that we can actually dwell there. And it becomes a place of:

INCREASED FAITH

*"If you abide in Me, and My words abide in you, ask whatever you wish, and **it shall be done** for you."*

JOHN 15:7

COMPLETE DELIVERANCE

*"For Thou hast tried us, O God; Thou hast refined us as silver is refined. Thou didst bring us into the net; Thou didst lay an oppressive burden upon our loins. Thou didst make men ride over our heads we went thru fire and thru water Thou didst **bring us out** into a place of abundance."*

PSALMS 66: 10-12

RESTORATION and REFRESHING

*"Wait on the Lord; be of good courage, and He **shall strengthen** thine heart: wait, I say, on the Lord!"*

PSALMS 27:14 NKJ

*" But they that wait upon the Lord shall **renew their strength**; they shall **mount up** with wings as eagles; they shall run and **not be weary**; and they shall walk and **not faint**."*

ISAIAH 40:31 KJ

*" He maketh me to lie down in green pastures: He leadeth me beside the still waters. **He restoreth** my soul: He leadeth me in the paths of righteousness for His name's sake."*

PSALMS 23:2, 3 KJ

TRIUMPH and REJOICING

"Because Thy loving-kindness is better than life, my **lips will praise Thee.** So I will **bless Thee** as long as I live; I will **lift up my hands** in Thy name.

My soul is satisfied as with marrow and fatness, and my mouth offers praises with **joyful lips.**

When I remember Thee on my bed, I meditate on Thee in the night watches, for Thou hast been my help, and in the shadow of Thy wings **I sing for joy.**

My soul clings to Thee; Thy right hand upholds me."

PSALMS 63:3-8

"But as for me, I shall **sing** of Thy strength; Yes, I shall **joyfully sing** of Thy loving kindness in the morning.

For Thou hast been my refuge in the day of distress...O my strength, I will **sing praises** to Thee..."

PSALMS 59:16

5
SUFFERING

REJOICE!

*"Count it **all joy**, my brethren, when you encounter various trials."*

JAMES 1:2

GREATLY REJOICE!

*"In this you **greatly rejoice**, even though now for a little while, if necessary, you have been distressed by various trials."*

I PETER 1:6

KEEP ON REJOICING!

*"Beloved, do not be surprised at the fiery ordeal among you, which comes upon you for your testing, as though some strange thing were happening to you; but to the degree that you share the sufferings of Christ, **keep on rejoicing**; so that also at the revelation of His glory, you may rejoice with exultation."*

I PETER 4;12

In this century, in this country, we look upon happiness and freedom from pain as part of our inalienable rights. Or as a reward for the person who manages his life well. Our worship of pleasure feeds this. So does our distorted view of the normal Christian life.

First century Christian thinking however, promised no such things. What they offered was a realistic lifestyle and it worked. Those to whom Peter wrote were objects of suspicion, hatred, severe scourgings and violence. But with assurance of their endless security in Christ, Peter exhorted them to *"greatly rejoice."* What consolation! Though surrounded by trials, the true believer in Christ can *always rejoice!*

The Lord Jesus spoke in John 16:33 KJ:

> "*These things have I spoken unto you, that in Me ye might have peace. In the world ye shall have tribulation, but **be of good cheer; I have overcome the world.***"

It could be translated: "cheer up."
God says, "'Whatever the circumstances – *rejoice!*"
Rejoice! even though we are suffering? Paradoxical!
How can one both rejoice and suffer at the same time?
First of all, IT IS POSSIBLE! But only to Christians.

The worldly-minded regard such a phenomenon as unnatural, unintelligible. The Stoic knows how to train himself to submit to inevitable fate; but the Christian possesses the "divine alchemy" by which sorrow may be turned into joy.

You see, joy and happiness are not the same…

Happiness depends on "happenings." But joy comes from the Lord.

JOY IS NEITHER
CIRCUMSTANTIAL OR CONSEQUENTIAL!

…because it is nourished by an unchanging source! The Scripture calls it *"unspeakable, full of glory."* In other words it is inexpressible in human language.

> *Joy is not the absence of suffering, but the presence of Christ.*

That is why the Apostle Paul could say:

> "*We are troubled on every side, yet not distressed, perplexed, but not in despair, persecuted, but not forsaken, cast down, but not destroyed.*"
>
> 2 CORINTHIANS 4:8, 9 KJ

GOOD REASONS TO REJOICE

1. TRIAL SHOWS US OUR OWN HEART.

Jeremiah tell us:

> "*The heart is deceitful…who can know it?*"
>
> JEREMIAH 17:9 KJ

"Who can discern his errors?"

PSALMS 19:12

"Every man's way is right in his own eyes, but the Lord weighs the hearts."

PROVERBS 21:2

You and I are unable to examine ourselves by introspection because our hearts are corrupt and inevitably we will be deceived. For instance: we may be wrong, yet our heart will justify us. Or we may be only weak, yet our hearts will condemn us as though we were wrong. Were our heart perfect, it could serve as a standard. But since it is deceitful, we dare not trust it!

"And you shall remember all the way which the Lord you God has led you in the wilderness these 40 years, that He might humble you, testing you, to know what was in your heart, whether you would keep His commandments or not."

DEUTERONOMY 8:2

So God uses trial and affliction to show a man "all that is in his heart."

"Search me, O God, and know my heart; Try me and know my anxious thoughts; And see if there be any hurtful way in me, And lead me in the everlasting way."

PSALMS 139: 23, 24

2. TRIAL PURIFIES OUR FAITH

Peter says, *"it is necessary"* to see if your faith is genuine. I Peter 1:6

To God, your faith is all-important

"…that the proof of your faith, being more precious than gold, which is perishable, even though tested by fire, may be found to result in praise and glory and honor at the revelation of Jesus Christ."

I PETER 1:7

Why?

Your whole relationship with Him hinges on that. This we learn from Hebrews 11:6

"And without faith it is impossible to please Him, for he who comes to God must believe that He is, and that He is a rewarder of those who seek Him."

Why Faith? Why not Courage, Love, Holiness?

Because it is foundational. All stands or falls *on faith*. Only trials reveal the deep resources and the reality of one's profession. Jewelers, we're told, have a method of determining the genuineness of a diamond. Place it in water and if it is real, it will reflect even a greater brilliance. But, if it's an imitation, the luster will grow dull. So the deep waters of trial reveal the believer's genuine beauty.

*FAITH MUST BE TESTED, TRIED AND PURIFIED…*to remove the things in which we put our trust, so we can clearly see the faithfulness of God.

WHAT IS FAITH?

It is "divine activity" within the human spirit.

It is a combination of two important faculties; *SEEING AND HEARING*

But not with our natural eyes and ears;

FAITH SEES THE INVISIBLE. Faith is the *EYE WHICH SEES.* God is a *SPIRIT* and the things of God are *SPIRITUAL.*

Andrew Murray says it well: "Faith depends upon our living in the invisible world."

The Bible speaks of varying degrees of faith: – *"little, weak, or great."*

HOW DO WE GET IT?
WHERE DOES IT COME FROM?

It comes to us from God in the *"gift of life!"* There is a fountain within. To every man is given a measure.

HOW DOES IT WORK?

By instinct it moves towards its *SOURCE.*

Does a mother need to give her daughter a course in "How to Fall in Love?" Of course not! It's in her nature. As a foal turns its face to the one who produces it…as a lamb to its ewe, so is faith inherent within our nature.

But all faculties need nourishment and environment.

FAITH GROWS BY FEEDING AND EXERCISE.

So, Faith by its very nature must be tried..

TRIAL REMOVES THE THINGS IN WHICH WE PUT OUR TRUST, SO WE CAN CLEARLY SEE THE FAITHFULNESS OF GOD.

> *Faith is not a "bridge over troubled waters," but a pathway thru them.*

Why must disappointments come to my life?

Why must I face unexpected trials, tribulations?

Why must my plans and hopes be blasted?

Peter assures us:

Trials are necessary — we can't get along without them — to see if your faith is genuine!

Andre Crouch said it well in his song:

"Thru it all…Thru it all,
I've learned to trust in Jesus,
I've learned to trust in God.
Thru it all…Thru it all,
I've learned to depend upon His word.

So I'll thank Him for the mountains,
And I'll thank Him for the valleys,
I'll thank Him for the storm He's brought me through;

For if I never had a problem,
I'd never know how He could solve them,
I'd never know what faith in God could do." [1]

> *"There is no pit so deep, but He is deeper still."*
>
> *Corrie ten Boom —*
> *"The Hiding Place"*

GOOD WORDS

God is so good to give us encouragement through words written and spoken by friends just when we need them most. Such came from our late friend, Bob Pierce, the founder of *WORLD VISION* and later *THE SAMARITAN'S PURSE.*

The call came late at night from City of Hope Hospital, Los Angeles. Speaking from a hospital bed in a very weak voice:

"Charles and Betty, I know what you are going through. This dying with leukemia is nothing, compared to dying to *self*." He continued to admonish from Hebrews 10:35,36: *"Therefore, do not cast away your confidence...For you have need of endurance..."*

For the next hour he preached from the text; and his voice became stronger with every word. But, those words became *"spirit and life"* to me and a *lifeline* to steer us through those dark days.

• • • • • • • • • • • • • • • •

From a colleague in the ministry came these encouraging words:

To my special friend, Charles Blair, whose life fulfills every aspect of this poem:

"IF"
"If you can keep your head when all about you
Are losing theirs and blaming it on you;
If you can trust yourself when all men doubt you,
But make allowance for their doubting too;
If you can wait and not be tired by waiting,
Or being lied about, don't deal in lies;
Or being hated, don't give way to hating,
And yet don't look too good, nor talk too wise;

If you can dream — and not make dreams your master;
If you can think — and not make thoughts your aim,
If you can meet with Triumph and Disaster
And treat those two imposters just the same;
If you can bear to hear the truth you've spoken
Twisted by knaves to make a trap for fools,
Or watch the things you gave your life to, broken,
And stoop and build 'em up with worn-out tools;

If you can make one heap of all your winnings
And risk it on one turn of pitch-and-toss
And lose, and start again at your beginnings
And never breathe a word about your loss;

If you can force your heart and nerve and sinew
To serve your turn long after they are gone,
And so hold on when there is nothing in you
Except the Will which says to them: 'Hold on!'

If you can talk with crowds and keep your virtue
Or walk with kings — nor lose the common touch
If neither foes nor living friends can hurt you,
If all men count with you, but none too much;
If you can fill the unforgiving minute
With sixty seconds' worth of distance run,
Yours is the Earth and everything that's in it,
And — which is more — you'll be a Man, my son!"
– Kipling

One night I copied this verse on a little card and put it on my husband's pillow:

"You were tired out by the length of your road, Yet you did not say, 'It is hopeless,' You found renewed strength, Therefore you did not faint."

Isaiah 57: 10

3. TRIAL PERFECTS OUR CHARACTER

"When all kinds of trials and temptations crowd into your lives, my brothers, don't resent them as intruders, but welcome them as friends!

*Realize that they come to test your faith and to **produce in you the quality of endurance**. But let the process go on until that endurance is fully developed and you will find that you have become men of **mature character** with the right sort of independence."*

James 1:2 (Phillips)

> *TRIALS Are not meant to take the strength out of us, but to put the strength into us.*

*"And after you have suffered for a little while, the God of all grace, who called you to His eternal glory in Christ, will Himself **perfect**, establish, strengthen, and settle you."*

I Peter 5:10

This is the end which God has in view in all His dealings with His people. He wants them to be *"perfect and entire."* God's way in the law of Christian suffering is that God will *restore, stablish, strengthen.* Each word here is a vivid picture telling us something about which suffering will do for us.

a.) *"restore"* is like setting a fracture-to supply that which is missing. It can repair the weaknesses and add to a man's character that which is lacking — adding the greatness that is not there.

This story is told of Sir Edward Elgar: the knighted English composer was asked to listen to a young girl singing a solo from one of his own works. She had a voice of exceptional purity and clarity and range, a voice like that of a boy soprano. She had an almost perfect technique which made light of the technical difficulties of the composition. When she had finished singing, Sir Edward said softly, "She will be really great when something happens to break her heart."

Robert Barrie speaks of his mother when she lost her favorite son....

"That is where my mother got her soft eyes...and that is why other mothers ran to her when they had lost a child."

SUFFERING HAD DONE SOMETHING FOR HER
THAT THE EASY WAY COULD NEVER HAVE DONE.

So, suffering is meant by God to add the grace notes to life.

In my Bible this poem –

"I asked the Lord that He should give success,
To the high task I sought for Him to do;
I asked that far and lofty heights be scaled.
And now I humbly thank Thee that I failed.

For with the pain and sorrow came to me
A dower of tenderness in act and thought
An insight which success had never brought.
Father, I had been foolish and unblest
If Thou hadst granted my blind request."

-Selected (Unknown)

"IF WE WOULD ALWAYS BE CHANGING OUR CIRCUMSTANCES
TO FIT OUR DESIRES,
WE WOULD PERISH OF SPIRITUAL DRY ROT."

J. Sidlow Baxter

"God is more interested in your character than your activity."

b.) Through suffering God will *"stablish"* a man. The word *"sterizein"* in the original means *"to make firm and solid as granite."* So suffering does one or two things:

> ….make him collapse or
> ….make a solidity of character

So then, we are not only strengthened *for,* but *by* suffering; and one of God's ways of *"stablishing"* us is to cut away all other props-that we may lean all our weight upon Him. He wants us to know Him!

"How can we trust a God we don't know? And how can we love a God we can't trust?"

c.) Peter also says God will *"strengthen"* in the furnace of affliction. The great preacher Spurgeon said: "The *'REFINER'* is never far from the mouth of the furnace when the gold is in the fire and the Son of God always is walking the midst of the flames when His holy children are cast in them."

Watchman Nee: "This is what is known as 'enlargement through pressure.' When three are shut into the furnace, and three become four-that is called 'enlargement through pressure.'" [2]

d.) God will *"settle."* It means to lay a foundation, It is when we are driven to the very bedrock of our faith and we discover what is really important in life. It is then we can distinguish between mere decorations and the basic essentials. It is *"removing those things which can be shaken…in order that those things which cannot be shaken may remain."* Hebrews 12:27

OUR FIERY TRIAL

During a real testing time in our life, God allowed another "fiery trial" to refine and purify. It came in the form of seeing our home literally go up in flames.

From the pastor's office, we heard the fire truck and sirens and my husband jokingly told someone on the phone: "I think our house is on fire." But it wasn't a joke. As I ran the short block, I was aghast to see smoke pouring from the second-story windows and the big fire hoses spouting water everywhere. The beautiful old Tudor home was owned by the church, but we were living there temporarily. We sat on the lawn, watching in utter amazement. Finally, just after the midnight hour a fireman stood at the front entrance and said:

"The fire is out — however, you cannot stay here – no electricity, no windows, no heat. But you can come in now and get your valuables."

At that moment, the Lord did a number on me! I stood there thinking, "Let's see now, what are my valuables?" It was a defining moment in my life.

The scene could have been from the movie, *Dr. Zhivalgo* – only done in black! Instead of snow and icicles, it was charcoal smoke and strips of curtains dripping with water. I was just sick at heart.

There is a kind of pain that accompanies the loss of things that are precious – whether it's voluntary or involuntary. Our daughters' wedding dresses were smoked to a crisp, still on the hangers in the cedar closet. The beautiful fabrics that my husband had brought me from the Far East lay smoldering in their boxes in the sewing room.

Many of our favorite books were blackened beyond repair. And, can you believe it – that very day, I had placed a lovely floral arrangement on the living room coffee table, as the final touch to a five-month project of remodeling and redecorating the whole house?

It was enough to make you cry — I mean, really cry!

Feeling a bit stunned, but thinking: "Lord, what is this?" Then I remembered those words which I uttered not many days before: "Lord, I want to come to the place where I can say, like David, 'I adore *all* Your ways.'

But this, Lord,..is this one of Your ways?" I'm sure that when David prayed "*Teach me Your Ways*," he never dreamed how God would do it. But when God teaches, the lesson sticks!

It is in life's trials that we discover the great truths on which life is founded and which we cannot do without.

It is then, we can distinguish between things that are mere decorations and those that are basic essentials — in other words, "What are our valuables?"

We were three months cleaning up the smoke damage; but some things were left with smoke stain (partly because I was exhausted), but also to remind me just how temporary and shakable "things" can be. I could even look at *House Beautiful* magazine now and through my tears of surrender, say: "It's O.K., Lord…You are more precious than silver."

One of the verses of the hymn, HOW FIRM A FOUNDATION reads:

> "When thru fiery trials thy pathway shall lie,
> My grace, all sufficient shall be thy supply;
> The flames shall not hurt thee: I only design
> Thy dross to consume, and thy gold to refine,
> Thy dross to consume, and thy gold to refine.

How wonderful it is when the Lord gives us the encouragement just at the time we need it through the writings and music of others. Often I would recall those words from my devotional, *TABLE IN THE WILDERNESS*:

"Behold we call them blessed which endured." James 5:11

"When God takes it in hand to deal with a man, He does not leave him till He has brought him through to a clear place. In His dealings with Job, God was characteristically thorough. He first allowed all his cattle to be carried off. Then his herds were consumed by fire. Next his sons and daughters died; and he had not yet emerged from his trials when, still protesting, he lay covered with "sore boils from the sole of his foot unto his crown."

But a day came when, in his utter subjection to God, Job's protests were silenced and God Himself was free to speak. Then at last his trials issued in final triumph. James refers to this as "the end of the Lord". Clearly therefore *what matters is not the number of our trials, but that we reach God's goal through them."* [3]

I was looking for my notes to a message the Lord gave me earlier, entitled: *"Singing In the Fire."* When I discovered them in my night stand, they were pretty well blackened by the smoke of our house fire and I thought: "Well, let's see — we've been through the flood — and the fire — and the court trial. All that is left now is the boils!"

Dan Burgess speaks of God's furrowing deep into the soil of men's hearts and planting a divine new hybrid crop — a sturdy strain that has been conceived in adversity and nourished in hope. And out of his own experience he wrote a song which became my theme song for many months. It is entitled simply:

PRESS ON

When the valley is deep, When the mountain is steep,
When the body is weary, When we stumble and fall; —
When the choices are hard, When we're battered and scarred,
When we've spent our resources, When we've given our all —
   In Jesus' name we press on, In Jesus' name we press on;
   Dear Lord, with the prize…clear before our eyes,
   We find the strength to press on. [4]

"A delicately balanced Christian spirit is not the result of a smooth, unruffled life!"
–Corrie ten Boom

ONE 'DARK NIGHT OF THE SOUL'

During the time when our world seemed to be crashing all around us, my husband experienced an assault of the powers of darkness upon his mind and body as never before. In the middle of the night he found himself face down upon the floor, clinging to the leg of the desk in his study, struggling for his very breath, inwardly crying out to God for help. He felt as though he was literally suffocating to death.

His heart was saying: "O God, let Betty come and pray for me!"

Moments later, he relates, "she was there beside me, praying the prayers I was struggling to utter. Then, amazingly, she began reading from the book that just 'happened to be' one of our class studies at the time, *THE SPIRITUAL MAN,* by Watchman Nee."

As I (Betty) was reading aloud to him from the chapter, "The Battlefield of the Mind,"— how the enemy unrelentingly seeks to attack the mind with thoughts of suicide, condemnation and defeat — sending them to your head in waves, that roll unceasingly day and night. As I read, he would cry out, "That's it! That's it! That's it!"

But, praise God, there was another chapter following entitled, "The Way of Deliverance." We began to recognize the spiritual war taking place in the mind and that our warfare was not *"against flesh and blood, but against principalities and powers of darkness."* Therefore worldly weapons would not do. We needed weapons that were *God – empowered "mighty in God for the pulling down of strongholds."* (2Corinthians 10:4) And then, to *"take captive every thought"* that is hostile to God. (v.5)

We also learned that *"The Word of God is living and powerful."* (Hebrews 4:12) And that when facing a situation of need, trial or difficulty, the promises of God may become *rhema* to you – that is, a living and powerful message, that goes deep into your soul. And that calls forth faith and hope…and courage! The words of Jesus are absolutely true — *"The words that I speak to you are spirit, and they are life."* John 6:63

It is these kind of experiences that cause us to grow spiritually. Such growth is painful because one undergoes stretching, molding, and refining by the Holy Spirit. But God wants His leaders to depend entirely on Him for their direction and empowering in the ministry. So it is for *our* profit and *His* glory that we are being trained by it. (Hebrews 12:11)

"And you shall remember that the Lord your God led you all the way these forty years in the wilderness, to humble you and test you, to know what was in your heart, whether you would keep His commandments or not.

So He humbled you, allowed you to hunger, and fed you with manna which you did not know nor did your fathers know, that He might make you know that man shall not live by bread alone; but man lives by every word that proceeds from the mouth of the Lord."

DEUTERONOMY 8:2

On my kitchen wall hangs this water-stained poem, penned by one of my dear pals who helped clean up the mess after the fire:

ONE ANSWER TO THE PRAYER
June 25, 1974

It was just about five weeks ago
That you stood and heard the sirens blow,
Peering out into the night;
Nearing was the engine's light.

You unlocked the door to see the smoke pour,
And the men grabbed their masks to begin the task;
While you were waiting for crews to come clean
You had to snooze in room 317.

For a bit of assistance you looked to the Pastor,
But all he could say was: 'Move a little faster.'
From that point on you had to rush;
So, many times you forgot your brush.

SERVICEMASTER…Knocking plaster…
Scrubbing walls, and cleaning halls.
We had never seen much, if anything, sadder
Than the painter standing, just holding the ladder.

Several people had a good plan:
Bringing in food to feed the clan.
I even know you had some trouble

Trying to determine what was in the rubble.

Some interruptions gave you fits, like:
A lost dog, millers, and birthday gifts.
A few things bothered you 'really good',
...Looking for the bills to Briarwood

Some of your friends were 'all in a dither'
Trying to find your brand new scissors.
You were not free, and yet it was vital
To read Watchman Nee and study your Bible.
Many days with not much rest
Yet, you know, this is just another TEST!
— Friend Marti

"Happy is he
who has the God of Jacob
for his help.
Whose hope is in the Lord
his God."

Psalm 146:5

6

THE FUTURE
(The Unknown)

"Oh…God…it hurts."

The pain in my heart was even greater than the cry in my voice.

The intercession was for our grandson, Brian, who had disappeared without a clue. Being a child of divorce, he has made his home with us much of his life. So I knew him well. Though now in his twenties, his life has been a struggle, complicated also by a learning disability.

> *'For I know the plans that I have for you declares the Lord, plans for good and not evil, to give you a future and a hope.'*
> *Jeremiah 29:11*

As the days increased, so did our concerns. I felt he would have returned, or called, if he were able. Without a job, or a car, or close friends, he was not easy to track. So we enlisted the help of police and posters, declaring him a "missing person." As the days passed into months, I felt he had become a victim of foul-play and possibly no longer alive. But where? I took the out-of-way roads, looking in empty lots and fields. Then someone reported that he might be doing the "homeless thing. "Oh…no! This is too much!"

My prayers became supplications…and my supplications became travail. I was experiencing those words of Andrew Murray: "True love must pray. It is the love of a mother for her prodigal son that makes her pray for him. The true love in us will become the spirit of intercession." Finally, the only thing I could do was to place him in the arms of Jesus and trust in His promises. And there were several of those, well-marked and dated in my Bible just for him:

"I have seen his ways, but I will heal him;
I will lead him and restore comfort to him and to his mourners."   ISAIAH 57:18

"For I will contend with the one who contends with you,
and I will save your sons."   ISAIAH 49:25B

"And all your sons will be taught of the Lord;
And the well-being of your sons will be great."   ISAIAH 54:13

And in that prayer of relinquishment, God gave me this word:

"Wherever Brian was, or is, My love preceded him there!"

Then, even through my tears, I could sing:

"Shepherd of love, You knew I had lost my way,
Shepherd of love, You cared that I'd gone astray.
You sought and found me, placed around me
Strong arms that carried me home;
No foe can harm me or alarm me — Never again will I roam!
Shepherd of love, Savior and Lord and Guide,
Shepherd of love, Forever I'll stay by Your side."

I found great comfort in Ruth Graham's poem:

"Sometimes I think it harder, Lord,
To cast the cares of those I love on You,
Than to cast mine.
But we, growing older, learn at last
That You are merciful and kind.
Not one time have you failed me, Lord —
Why do I fear that You'll fail mine?"

Brian Moore, Grandson

Then it happened – a phone call. He had been seen – walking not far from our home. I quickly phoned my daughter, Judi, who "happened to be" in her car in the very area, and I said, "Please look! …Right now!…he's alive!"

Within the hour, she had found him, behind a dumpster, counting his pennies. After some time, he consented to go home with her, and she became his "angel of mercy." Through her many weeks of persistent and untiring efforts, he received the help needed in counseling and support groups. God is truly faithful! He heard my cry and answered!

But now, every time I see a homeless person alongside the road, holding their cardboard signs, begging for help, I see them through different eyes – most of all, I pray for their deeper needs.

The saddest part is not that they are "homeless" or helpless, but that they are "hope-less." By that, I do not mean there is no hope for them; rather, I mean there is no hope *in* them. They must know that there is no future in what they are doing, but they lack the incentive to move up higher. They are without hope. It is a spiritual problem.

HOPE! We cannot live without it!

THEY ARE NOT ALONE.
OTHERS HAVE FELT THAT WAY:

I think of:

HAGAR
The single mother

Alone in the wilderness, fleeing and despondent, she is surprised by a heavenly visitor:

> *"And the angel of the Lord found her by a spring of water in the wilderness.....and said: "'Where have you come from? and where are you going?'"*
> GENESIS 16:7,8

JOB

> *"And where now is my **hope**? As for my **hope**, who shall see it?"*
> JOB 17:15 KJ

ZION

> *"The Lord hath **forsaken** me, and my Lord hath **forgotten** me."*
> ISAIAH 49:14 KJ

JONAH

*"...wished in himself to **die**, and said, it is better for me to die than to live."*

JONAH 4:8 KJ

JOHN, BAPTIST IN PRISON

"and said to Him, 'Are You the Coming One, or do we look for another?'"

MATTHEW 11:3 NKJ

UNBELIEVERS

*"That at that time ye were without Christ, being aliens from the commonwealth of Israel, and strangers from the covenants of promise, **having no hope**, and without God in the world."*

EPHESIANS 2:12 NKJ

GRIEVING SAINTS

*"But I would not have you to be ignorant, brethren, concerning them which are asleep, that ye sorrow not, as others who have **no hope!**"*

I THESSALONIANS 4:13 KJ

> 'A man who loses purpose in life is already dead.

*"**Hope** deferred makes the heart sick: but when desire comes, it is a tree of life."*

PROVERBS 13:12 NKJ

HOPE FOR THE HOPELESS.

For those who are "hope-less", God has provided a future worth hoping for — something far beyond our fondest dreams or expectations – and that hope, then, becomes an "anchor to the soul."

And that future begins with a quality of life now. Eternal life is not just a matter of *quantity*, but also *quality*. And that quality is enhanced and stimulated by the knowledge and understanding of *who you are* and *what you have been given*.

Namely, you have been given some very special titles:

CHILDREN OF GOD

*"The Spirit itself beareth witness with our spirit, that we are the **children of God**...delivered from the bondage of corruption into the glorious liberty of the children of God."*

ROMANS 8:16, 21, KJ

*"Neither can they die any more: for they are equal unto the angels; and are the **children of God**, being the children of the resurrection."*

LUKE 20:36, KJ

HEIRS OF GOD

*"And if children, then heirs; **heirs of God**, and joint heirs with Christ; if so be that we suffer with Him, that we may be also glorified together."*

ROMANS 8:17, KJ

*"And if ye be Christ's, then are ye Abraham's seed, and **heirs** according to the promise."*

GALATIANS 3:29, KJ

*"That being justified by His grace, we should be made **heirs** according to hope of eternal life."*

TITUS 3:7, KJ

*"In the same way God, desiring even more to show to the **heirs of the promise** the unchangeableness of His purpose, interposed with an oath, in order that by two unchangeable things, in which it is impossible for God to lie, we may have strong encouragement, we who have fled for refuge in laying hold of the **hope** set before us.*

*This **hope** we have as an anchor of the soul, **a hope** both sure and steadfast and one which enters within the veil."*

HEBREWS 6:17-19

SONS OF GOD

"But as many as received Him, to them gave He power to become the **sons of God**, *even to them that believe on His name."*

JOHN 1:12, KJ

"For as many as are led by the Spirit of God, they are the **sons of God***.'"*

ROMANS 8:14, KJ

"Wherefore thou art no more a servant, but a **son***; and if a* **son***, then an heir of God, through Christ."*

GALATIANS 4:7, KJ

"Behold, what manner of love the Father hath bestowed upon us, that we should be called the **sons of God***: therefore the world knoweth us not, because it knew Him not."*

I JOHN 3:1, KJ

CHOSEN

"….did not God choose the poor of this world to be rich in faith and heirs of the kingdom **which He promised to those who love Him***?"*

JAMES 2:5

"But you are a **chosen** *race, a royal priesthood, a holy nation. A people for God's own possession, that you may proclaim the excellencies of Him who has called you out of darkness into His marvelous light."*

I PETER 2 9

SONS OF LIGHT

"While ye have the light, believe in the light, in order that you may become **sons of light***."*

JOHN 12:36, KJ

"For you were once darkness, but now you are light in the Lord. Walk as **children of light.***"*

EPHESIANS 5:8, NKJ

"For ye are all **sons of light***, and* **sons of the day***. We are not of the night, nor of darkness: so then let us not sleep, as do the rest, but let us watch and be sober."*

I THESSALONIANS 5:5, KJ

LOVED AND CHOSEN

"Long ago, even before He made the world, God chose us to be His very own, through what Christ would do for us; He decided then to make us holy in His eyes, without a single fault – we who stand before Him covered with His love. His unchanging plan has always been to adopt us into His own family by sending Jesus Christ to die for us. And He did this **because He wanted to!***"*

EPHESIANS 1: 4, 5, TLB

*"...***So overflowing is His kindness towards us*** that He took away all our sins through the blood of His Son, by whom we are saved; and He has showered down upon us the richness of His grace – for how well He understands us and knows what is best for us at all times."*

VS.7,8

> 'The Devil has a terror plan, But God has a better plan!'

"….I pray that your hearts will be flooded with light so that you can see something of the **future He has called you to share***. I want you to realize that God has been made rich because we who are Christ's have been given to Him! I pray that you will begin to understand how incredibly great is His power to help those who believe Him. It is that same mighty power that raised Christ from the dead and seated Him in the place of honor at God's right hand in heaven, far, far above any other king or ruler or dictator or leader. Yes, His honor is far more glorious than that of anyone else, either in this world or in the world to come!"*

EPHESIANS 1:16-21, TLB

We fear the future because it is unknown. But God has provided all we need to know about the past and the future within His holy Word.

So He has provided for us both a FUTURE and a HOPE!

Our friend of years ago, Ira Stamphill, penned this song:

"I KNOW WHO HOLDS TOMORROW"

I don't know about tomorrow,

I just live from day to day;

I don't borrow from its sunshine,

For its skies may turn to gray;

I don't worry o'er the future,

For I know what Jesus said,

And today I'll walk beside Him,

For He knows what is ahead.

Many things about tomorrow

I don't seem to understand;

But I know who holds tomorrow,

And I know Who holds my hand.

Daughter Judi
(Brian's Angel)

7
DEATH

The fear of death is the master fear from which all other fears come. All worry, phobias, etc., stem from the fear of death. But we, as God's child, have been delivered from the source of terror and its oppression. We are no longer subject to it. In fact, we have been set free from the spiritual laws in which sin and death operate. Romans 8:2 tells us:

"For the law of the Spirit of life in Christ Jesus hath made me free from the law of sin and death."

It is said:

WE CANNOT REALLY LIVE UNTIL WE HAVE FACED OUR OWN DEATH.

When an aircraft breaks the sound barrier, it soars with freedom. Likewise when we break the death barrier, we can live triumphantly, knowing that when we die we are just entering the next phase of *"eternal life."*

THIS IS THE UNIQUE MESSAGE OF
CHRISTIANITY:
CHRIST HAS CONQUERED DEATH!

We no longer are slaves to this fear all our lives, but our shackles are knocked off and we are forever released. CAPTIVITY IS TAKEN CAPTIVE! Satan, who had the power of death, is now rendered powerless. Hebrews 2:14.15

The authentic mark of a Christian is both peace and joy in the face of life's problems – most of all, facing death.

"Since we, God's children, are human beings – made of flesh and blood – He became flesh and blood too by being born in human form; for only as a human being could He die and in dying, break the power of the devil who had the power of death. Only in that way could He deliver those who through fear of death have been living all their lives as slaves to constant dread."
Hebrews 2:14,15 TLB

121

A living example of this is seen in our dear, dear friends, Paul and Elaine Finch, missionaries to Italy for more than 20 years. In Elaine's four-year battle with cancer, they were persistent in their faith, experiencing God's grace in unlimited measure and through it all, ministering life to others in a most remarkable way.

A few excerpts from their letters:

Paul & Elaine Finch and daughter Loretta

Dec. '99': "The text God gave us in the context of this particular emergency was Isaiah 8:12-14 (NIV): "Do not call conspiracy everything that these people call conspiracy; do not fear what they fear, and do not dread it. The Lord Almighty is the one you are to regard as holy, He is the one you are to fear, He is the one you are to dread, and He will be a sanctuary."

The challenge to Israel in Isaiah's day was literally as to whom they were going to trust — their own political calculations or God and His promises. Put in the context of our present experiences it means

-   Are we now going to dread a future recurrence, since this is what the statistics of this particular disease tell us is likely to happen?

-   Or, are we going to trust God who is saying to us that although it might be legitimate, it would be wrong.

The human response of fear and dread, while following justifiable and rational calculation, are, in this particular case, wrong. We are to trust in Him, to fear Him, to dread Him, to regard Him as holy and to make Him our sanctuary. We are not good at this because we have so much admired the expertise of the doctors and know that their statistical calculations are very well founded. At the same time, it's so clear that God would have us live trusting and hoping in Him. That does not mean burying our head in the sands and thinking "Elaine-is-going-to-be-an-exception" (although there is no reason for thinking that she could not be so either. The medical knowledge available does not make a future recurrence inevitable – just probable.)

But it certainly does mean choosing to trust God with each future moment that God is so graciously giving. We are very privileged to have had such competent surgical help. God's bounty has surely been so generously ours. In every way it seems right to respond to God's kindness by trusting in Him.

So dear ones, as you thank God with us for such magnificent help (as we look at other situations in the hospital, it's almost too wonderful to believe at times!), please join hands with us in asking God to hold our hearts towards a steadfast gaze of Him. It's not natural, but it's so right!"

– Paul (for Elaine)

May 2001: 1½ years later:

"I am aware that the weakness is increasing all the time, reminding us that the overall situation has not changed and reminding us that my well-being is indeed an extra gift from God.

Thank you for all your fervent prayers. Many write to say that they are praying for complete healing. We believe God could well do that even at this "impossible" stage, and we would be delighted! Even if God should heal fully however, we know it would not be a bigger miracle than what He has already done. It is humanly impossible for us to have such peace, hope and even joy while living through such a sad and stressful situation. Yet God is performing exactly this miracle, to his glory. True, tears are there, frequently so, and anxiety knocks at our heart's door regularly. Death seems to be entering our family, threatening to change everything permanently. This is countered, however by God drawing us gently into his presence and whispering:

> 'You are my child by grace through your faith in the sufficiency of Jesus' death to pay for your sin.
> Therefore I am here and will always remain with you to carry and care for you no matter what I bring into your life. That is my promise as written in My Word.'

In our experience up until now He has kept this promise. Surely He does not change. This truth, as we receive and believe it, gives us deep, deep comfort and joy – even a great hope for the future. Is that not a miracle, to God's glory?!!!

By all means, pray with us for healing but, most importantly, pray that we will be enabled to trust God's promises as made to each child of his. Future days may prove to be much harder than what we have gone through so far (which has been so graciously "smoothed over" and softened compared to what the reality of our situation would indicate)! Pray that our faith in Him not falter, thus dishonoring Him. That is our greatest concern.

What more can we say? We are humbled and delighted at God's abundant salvation! Thank you for sharing these unusually blessed ways of God with us. With our warmest greetings in Christ."

– Elaine

Nov. 2001:

"Dear ones, although some of you I will have spoken with by phone, perhaps it is appropriate to ask you all to pray for Elaine and myself.

Today seems to have confirmed that Elaine is now more on the side of heaven than that of earth. Although yesterday she ate a wonderful lunch, today she has slept all day and has not eaten anything. And I really can't awaken her to eat either. Although she has been awake for a few minutes on a few occasions throughout the day, she has always quickly dropped back into a deep profound sleep. It's as though she is slipping out of life into heaven.

While on the one hand I am delighted for her, it is very hard for me to embrace her joyous arrival at the end of life's pilgrimage, and waves of grief wash over me almost sweeping me off my feet. To cry is not wrong, and to experience deep grief is right, love could not be otherwise. However, the struggle is to not let that same depth of emotion become the focus to the extent that the Lord of hosts is no longer my place of refuge. And it's from that perspective that I ask you to pray – that I may fear Him more than my future alone, that I may genuinely sanctify Him in my heart. I sense that this is what God is wanting of me. Mine is to embrace Him and His choices but I'm discovering just how fragile I am and ask you to pray for me and my loved ones. Thanks so much."

– In Christ, Paul

Elaine went to be with the Lord very peacefully on Saturday November 24, 2001.

January, 2002

"It's amazing that more than 6 weeks have gone by since that unforgettable Saturday evening when Elaine slipped from life into God's glorious presence. Although we had thought through most of the various details which would have to be sorted out following her death, while she was with me we never felt free to actually proceed with anything. We always felt that the proper way to wait was not for her death, but rather to wait on God.

Although it seemed that God was not giving healing, we never felt that her cancer was in charge. The text from Psalm 16, *'Lord, you have assigned me my portion and my cup,; You have made my lot secure. The boundary lines have fallen for me in pleasant places; surely I have a delightful inheritance'* was a constant encouragement to us both.

In a strange way, although each day was filled with medical necessities, somehow we felt that God would have us fully trust in Him — right to the end, whatever He might be pleased to give us.

Perhaps the hardest but most important challenge of all has been that of the daily, moment by moment, necessity to choose to emotionally trust in God.

There are many, many occasions when I deeply miss Elaine. It's almost as though half of me is missing. Quite suddenly tears flood up from the depths of my person as I realize that my dearest friend on earth is gone forever. Sometimes it seems as though I could cry forever. And yet, were I to allow those thoughts to build on one another, I know that in all probability I would drift ever closer to depression and despair and to do that would be to not appreciate all God gave us.

Somehow, my focus must be on God Himself and my life with Him rather my life without Elaine. After all, He is the one who gave me such a lovely wife. Without Him we would never have enjoyed such a union. He blessed us, gave us 34 wonderful years, and helped us learn to love one another.

Our last 4 years, although physically limited by Elaine's medical needs, were, in many ways, the richest. To think that God has now abandoned me would be wrong! He who was the giver, still remains the giver — and mine is to keep on trusting His promise that His *"love is better than life."* Psalm 63

...Your prayers have been a vital life-line to God for me. I see increasingly how God wants faith to be a verb rather than a noun — a continuous choice to trust Him for every detail!

From my heart, I thank you all for your help and love."

– In Christ, Paul

These words read like a modern-day Epistle. They speak to us with great force, as we see a living example of faith that does not falter, even in the face of death. Truly, these two lives have inspired many to *"seek after"* and *"lay hold"* on a greater faith and a greater knowledge of God's unlimited grace and power. They might well be listed along with the heroes of faith in Hebrews 11, demonstrating the truth that:

DEATH MAY SEIZE A BELIEVER, BUT CANNOT STING HIM — CANNOT HOLD HIM IN HIS POWER!

Christ, by dying, has taken out this sting. He has made atonement for it; He has obtained remission of it. It may hiss, but it cannot hurt!

*"**Thanks be to God, who gives us the victory through our Lord Jesus Christ!**"*

I CORINTHIANS 15:57

FEAR NOTS FOR DEATH

*"Even though I walk thru the valley of the shadow **of death**, I fear no evil; for **Thou art with me**, Thy rod and Thy staff they comfort me."*

PSALMS 23:4

*"For God so loved the world that he gave his only begotten son, that whosoever believeth in him **should not perish**, but have everlasting life."*

JOHN 3:16 KJ

*"Truly, truly, I say to you, If a man keep my word, he shall **never see death**."*

JOHN 8:51 KJ

"I am the resurrection and the life: he who believes in Me though he may die, he shall live...Do you believe this?"

JOHN 11:25,26 NKJ

*"The last enemy that shall be destroyed is **death**."*

I Corinthians 15:26 KJ

"For as in Adam all die, so also in Christ all shall be made alive."

I Corinthians 15:22

*"But when this perishable will have put on the imperishable, and this mortal will have put on immortality, then will come about the saying that is written: **"DEATH IS SWALLOWED UP IN VICTORY."***

I Corinthians 15:54

*"...and the dead in Christ **shall rise** first. Then we who are alive and remain shall be caught up together with them in the clouds to meet the Lord in the air, and thus shall we ever be with the Lord."*

I Thessalonians 4:16, 17

*"But now has been revealed by the appearing of our Savior Christ Jesus, who **abolished death**, and brought life and immortality to light through the gospel."*

II Timothy 1:10

*"Fear not; I am the first and the last: I am he that liveth, and was dead; and behold, I am **alive** forevermore, Amen; and have the keys of hell and death."*

Revelation 1: 17,18 KJ

*"And God shall wipe away every tear from their eyes; and there shall be **no more death**, neither sorrow nor crying, neither shall there be any more pain, for the former things are passed away."*

Revelation 21:4 KJ

Eternal Life

Lord, make me an instrument of Thy peace:

Where there is hatred, let me sow love,

Where there is injury, pardon;

Where there is doubt, faith,

Where there is dispair, hope;

Where there is sadness, joy.

O Divine Master, grant

That I may not so much seek

To be consoled as to console,

To be understood as to understand,

To be loved as to love;

For it is in giving that we receive;

It is in pardoning that we are pardoned;

It is in dying that we are born to eternal life!

St. Francis of Assisi

Part Three:

FACING FEAR

"Who shall separate us from the love of Christ? Shall tribulation, or distress, or persecution, or famine, or nakedness, or peril, or sword?... Nay in all these things we are more than conquerors through Him who loved us. For I am persuaded that neither death, nor life, nor angels, nor principalities, nor powers, nor things to come, nor height, nor depth, nor any other creature, shall be able to separate us from the love of God, which is in Christ, Jesus Our Lord."

Romans 8:35-39

"There is no fear in love, but perfect love casts out fear because fear involves torment. But he who fears has not been made perfect in love."

I John 4:18

"The Lord is my Light and my Salvation. Whom, then shall I fear? The Lord is the Strength of my life: of whom, then shall I be afraid?

Psalm 27:1

"Love Never Fails."

1 Corinthians 13:8

1
THE KNOCK-OUT BLOW:
Love

It has been called

THE GREATEST FORCE IN THE UNIVERSE.

It is as fixed as the law of gravity, as durable as time, and as lasting as eternity. It is God's greatest gift to man and it is man's greatest need.

It is called *PERFECT LOVE!*

It is that which keeps life from becoming a barren treadmill, stripped of all creative action and joy.

It's the ingredient that gives life meaning and purpose.
Babies have died for lack of it,
> Men have fought to gain or preserve it.
> > And God gave His only Son because of it.

> *"Perfect Love casts out Fear."*
> *I John 4:18*

To even begin to comprehend or fathom this truth is like a child reaching for a star. Still, as I stretch my heart toward that awesome, wonder-filled theme, I am filled with everything good.

WHO NEEDS IT?

The truth is we cannot live without LOVE! It has been called the "guardian of life" because without it we lose the will to live.

Dr. Smiley Blanton, M.D., well-known author and psychiatrist, explains:

"Most people understand love to mean simply love between the sexes. It does mean this, but also much more. On the deepest level, love is an instinctive force present in every person from birth to death. It is a profound urge to preserve and extend life by means of union with another living force, and it expresses itself through an exchange of energy that mutually strengthens and rejuvenates.

Love is born when the child rests in its mother's arms. From this beginning, love grows until it includes the love of family and friends, of school and country, and ultimately of all the world. Love also means love of self. This is an aspect often ignored, yet it is of basic importance — for without healthy self-love, one cannot love anyone else. Love also means love of God, a love that sustains us when human relationships crumble.

Love is all of one piece — from the love of mother and child to the love of sweethearts, husbands and wives, and friends. It is present, too, in the laborer's devotion to his work, in the teacher's solicitude for her pupils, in the physician's dedication to his art. All that heals, cultivates, protects, and inspires — all this is a part of love.

To say that one will perish without love does not mean that everyone without adequate love dies. Many do, for without love the will to live is often impaired to such an extent that a person's resistance is critically lowered and death follows. But most of the time, lack of love makes people depressed, anxious and without zest for life. They remain lonely and unhappy, without friends or work they care for, their life a barren treadmill, stripped of all creative action and joy."

He continues: "When we cannot give and receive love freely, we become easy prey to the dread emotions of fear and resentment, of anxiety and guilt. These diverse expressions of hostility so distort our outlook that we are then unable to view life in a clear and objective manner. FEAR paralyzes our natural impulses to explore and investigate, while resentment causes us to misinterpret what we see. Anxiety prevents us from accepting the normal experiences whereby we grow and develop to our full potentialities. Guilt, in turn, forces us to punish ourselves with accidents and faulty actions that lead to unnecessary frustration and defeat.

Against these hostile emotions neither laws nor logic can prevail. They hurtle us on to repeated errors despite ourselves — for LOVE is the only true source of knowledge, and without it we lose our ability to learn and to understand. Nothing can stop the spiral except LOVE!" [1]

"And now abide faith, hope, love, these three; but the greatest of these is LOVE."

I CORINTHIANS 13:13

HOW CAN I KNOW IT?

Love has its origin in God. It is from the God who *is* love that all love takes its source. *"...for love is from God; and everyone who loves is born of God and knows God...for God is love."* (I John 4:7, 8). He is the fountain, author, parent, commander of love. The Spirit of God is the spirit of LOVE.

If God is love, it means that God cannot exist in lonely isolation. Love, to be love, must have someone to love, and someone to love it. God's act of creation was a necessity of His divine nature, because being love, it was necessary for God to have someone whom He might love, and who might love Him.

In the words of Rufus Moseley: "The only possible way for God to be God (Love) and remain God (Love) was for Him to love us and love the universe into loving."[2]

So God Himself is the "Originator" and the "Source" — the "Great Designer" and because He is LOVE, He can do no less than create something beautiful and good. Genesis 1: 10, 12, 18, 21

Thus begins "THE GREATEST STORY EVER TOLD" with God's plan of the ages in creation, redemption and restoration of man, the object of His divine love.

I especially love to read Ephesians 1 from the new translation, THE MESSAGE:

"How blessed is God! And what a blessing He is! He's the Father of our Master, Jesus Christ, and takes us to the high places of blessing in Him. Long before He laid down earth's foundations, He had us in mind, had settled on us as the focus of His love, to be made whole and holy by His love. Long,

long ago He decided to adopt us into His family through Jesus Christ. (What pleasure He took in planning this!)

He wanted us to enter into the celebration of His lavish gift-giving by the hand of His beloved Son.

Because of the sacrifice of the Messiah, His blood poured out on the altar of the Cross, we're a free people — free of penalties and punishments chalked up by all our misdeeds. And not just barely free, either. Abundantly free! He thought of everything, provided for everything we could possibly need, letting us in on the plans He took such delight in making. He set it all out before us in Christ, a long-range plan in which everything would be brought together and summed up in Him, everything in deepest heaven, everything on planet earth.

It's in Christ that you, once you heard the truth and believed it (this Message of your salvation), found yourselves home free — signed, sealed, and delivered by the Holy Spirit. This signet from God is the first installment on what's coming, a reminder that we'll get everything God has planned for us, a praising and glorious life."

EPHESIANS 1:3-14

LOVE MUST ACT

Those of us who are mothers especially understand this principle —

LOVE CANNOT BE QUIESCENT.

It must express itself in giving to those we love. And we are forever thinking of ways to express this, consciously or unconsciously.

When our girls were small I would hire my housework done and spend my time sewing organdy pinafores with ruffles to make my little darlings beautiful — because I loved it! It was simply a natural expression of my mother heart. And it continued, even after they were grown.

Vicki & Judi – "Organdy Ruffles

While our daughter and husband were stationed in Germany and expecting their first-born, Marrles, I decided to make two maternity dresses and send them to her. I spent hours creating and sewing and they were gorgeous! One was a powder blue knit with four sparkling rhinestone buttons at the yoke. The other, a paisley print in autumn colors, Chinese style. With excitement and motherly devotion, I wrapped and mailed them; and with great expectance I waited…and waited…and waited.

But there was no response.

Then I began to wonder: "That ungrateful child! I'll never do a thing for her again!" But softly I heard a little voice say: "O yes, you will…yes, you will." And then, it seems the Lord whispered in my ear: "How many times have I done something for you, and I waited…and waited…and waited…and yet, there was no response from you."

The end of that story is: She never received the package. It was destroyed in a Postal Office Building fire on the East Coast.

And that wasn't the end of my sewing, either!

It is the nature of LOVE to be active, creative and benign. So where love is, love must ever give to its own, whatever the cost. God demonstrated His love to us in Jesus Christ. It is in Jesus that we see fully displayed the love of God. It is the love which holds nothing back — He sent his only Son.

> *"God commendeth His love toward us, in that, while we were yet sinners, Christ died for us."*
> ROMANS 5:8

> *"God so loved the world, that He gave His only begotten Son."*
> JOHN 3:16 KJ

This love content is that which distinguishes Christianity from all other religions, and elevates it to heights far beyond even the purest and noblest philosophy. Zephaniah 3:10 tells us that God Himself is in the midst of His Church singing over His people.

And our response to the Lord's love song is, also, one of joy and praise.

In the words of Andre Crouch:

"How can I say thanks
for the things You have done for me —
Things so undeserved,
Yet You give to prove Your love for me?
The voices of a million angels could not express my gratitude —
All that I am and ever hope to be,
I owe it all to Thee.
To God be the glory, To God be the glory,
To God be the glory for the things He has done.
With His blood He has saved me,
With His power He has raised me;
To God be the glory for the things He has done." [3]

LOVE'S RESPONSE

"We love, because He first loved us." I John 4:19

His love is the *incentive — the motivating force — the cause of ours.* We *cannot but love so good a God, who was first in the act and work of love.* The true Christian is one who has accepted this invitation and believes this love.

Because it was He —

- who loved us when we were both unloving and unlovely. Roman 5:6-8

- who loved us at so great an expense of His Son's blood.
  John 10:11; Revelation 5:9

- who never stops seeking and wooing us unto Himself.
  Lamentations 3:22, 23

The true Christian *knows* and *believes* this love. Some may talk of it — even quoting Scripture, but it is the Christian alone who truly apprehends it. And it can be recognized because it diffuses a loving warmth through the soul and causes every grace to flourish and abound. To a person who truly loves God, the thought of Him will be sweet to his soul; and the more intimate he feels his access to God, the greater will be his joy!

THE LIGHTED CHRISTIAN

Watchman Nee (*The Normal Christian Life*) refers to a sainted woman who impacted his life:

"If I did but walk into her room, I was brought immediately to a sense of God. In those days I was very young and had been converted about two years, and I had lots of plans, lots of beautiful thoughts, lots of schemes for the Lord to sanction, a hundred and one things which I thought would be marvelous if they were all brought to fruition. With all these things I came to her to try to persuade her; to tell her that this or that was the thing to do.

Before I could open my mouth, she would just say a few words in quite an ordinary way. Light dawned! It simply put me to shame, my "doing" and my scheming were all so natural, so full of man. Something happened. I was brought to a place where I could say: 'Lord, my mind is set only on creaturely activities, but here is someone who is not out for them at all. Teach me to walk that way.'

She had but one motive, one desire, and that was for God. Written in the front of her Bible were these words: 'Lord, I want nothing for myself.' Yes, she lived for God alone, and where that is the case you will find that such a one is bathed in light, and that light illuminates others. That is real witness." [4]

In the fly-leaf of my Bible are these poems:

A PERSIAN FABLE

One day a wanderer found a lump of clay
So redolent of sweet perfume,
Its odor scented all the room.
"What art thou?" was his quick demand;
"Art thou some gem from Sumarcand?
Then whence this wondrous perfume, I pray?"
"Friend, if the secret I disclose
I have been living with the Rose."

Sweet parable! And will not those

Who love to dwell with Sharon's Rose

Distil sweet odors all around

Tho low and mean themselves are found?

Dear Lord, may we to Thee retreat

Then shed abroad Thy fragrance sweet.

- Anonymous

Not only in the words you say,

Not only in your deeds expressed,

But in the most unconscious way

Is Christ expressed.

Is it in a beautific smile

A holy light upon your brow?

Oh no! I felt His presence

While you laughed just now.

For me 'twas not the truth you taught

To you so clear, to me so dim;

But when you came, you brought

A sense of Him.

And from your eyes He beckons me,

And from your heart his love is shed,

'Til I lose sight of you and see

The Christ instead.

- Anonymous

THAT DIVINE LOVE STAMPED LOVE UPON OUR SOULS
AND
DIRECTS OUR HEARTS FURTHER STILL INTO HIS LOVE.

II THESSALONIANS 3:5

– It will be the one subject of our meditations,
  – the one theme of our praises,
    – the one goal of our life.

THE WAY OF LOVE BECOMES A WAY OF LIFE.

The love of God and love of man are indissolubly connected. I John 4: 7, 11, 20, 21. The energy of love could be drawn in the form of a triangle, whose points are God, self, and neighbor. If God loves us, we are bound to love each other, because it is our destiny and our highest aim to reproduce the *life of God* in humanity, and the *life of eternity* in time.

Our good friend, E. Stanley Jones has said:

"When you surrender to Christ you surrender to *creative love*. And all you say, do and are is heightened by that impact. You think thoughts you couldn't think, you do things you couldn't do, you are a person you could not otherwise be. You are a surprise to yourself and others."

He adds: "The past is buried in the love of God, the present is guided by the love of God, and the future is unfolding under the beckoning of the love of God." [5]

No wonder it is called the "new birth" or being "born again!"

Again from THE MESSAGE, we read Paul's words from Colossians 3:1-14:

"So if you're serious about living this new resurrection life with Christ, act like it. Pursue the things over which Christ presides. Don't shuffle along, eyes to the ground, absorbed with the things right in front of you. Look up, and be alert to what is going on around Christ — that's where the action is. See things from His perspective.

Your old life is dead. Your new life, which is your real life — even though invisible to spectators — is with Christ in God. He is your life. When Christ (your real life, remember) shows up again on this earth, you'll show up, too — the real you, the glorious you. Meanwhile, be content with obscurity, like Christ.

Don't lie to one another. You're done with that old life. It's like filthy set of ill-fitting clothes you've stripped off and put in the fire. Now you're dressed in a new wardrobe. Every item of your new way of life is custom-made by the Creator, with His label on it. All the old fashions are now obsolete. Words like Jewish and non-Jewish, religious and irreligious, insider and outsider, uncivilized and uncouth, slave and free, mean nothing. From now on everyone is defined by Christ, everyone is included in Christ.

So, chosen by God for this new LIFE OF LOVE, dress in the ward-robe God picked out for you: compassion, kindness, humility, quiet strength, discipline. Be even-tempered, content with second place, quick to forgive an offense. Forgive as quickly and completely as the Master forgave you. And regardless of what else you put on, wear LOVE. IT'S YOUR BASIC, ALL-PURPOSE GARMENT. NEVER BE WITHOUT IT."

HOW DOES IT WORK?

When the *way of love* becomes our *way of life*, it is like a "Magnificent Obsession."

Every day becomes an exciting adventure looking for opportunities to "bless you in the Name of the Lord," and watch with expectancy for the changes that the Lord's blessing will accomplish in others. Each new day presents us with a world of ways to practice this. Sometimes it means taking time out to *love and play* with the "little ones." Sometimes it means making time to *love and pray* for the "big ones." But believe me, when you decide to commit to this, God will provide you with opportunities to test His proven law — the law of love.

In his book, *The Blessing*, Gary Smalley speaks of the power we can create in our children by our affirmation. He says that no matter what age you are, the approval of parents affects how your view yourself and your ability to pass that approval on to your children. Many people spend a lifetime

Betty & five grandchildren hiking in Colorado mountains

looking for this acceptance which the Bible calls *"the blessing."* And that "family blessing" is still done in Jewish families today. But in the Old Testament they used words to pronounce that blessing, and those words spoken gave the recipient a goal and a hope for the future. It was suggested that we select something the child relates to and call them by name such as Jacob did with his sons when He called Judah a *"lion's cub"* and Joseph *"a fruitful bough."* [6]

I was so excited to try it on my little granddaughter, Kelly. She was an effervescent little blue-eyed blonde with a sunny disposition and I would sing to her from Julie Andrews' *Sound of Music:*

> *"Do, a deer, a female deer,*
> *Re, a drop of golden sun,*
> *Mi, a name I call myself,*
> *Fa, a long, long way to run…."*

Kelly Lynn, granddaughter

Kelly

That fit her perfectly! I called her my "little golden ray of sun." "She would just glow with delight and we bonded immediately. I would also sing the song of Amy Grant's *You've Got Your Father's Eyes.* And it was wonderful to see the smile on her face, the childish giggle, and the light in those blue, blue eyes. That in itself was a blessing to me! And I'm certain that even though she's a grown woman today, she has not forgotten those precious times together.

Those are the moments that children remember and our words can picture not only who they are, but who they can become.

What, then, is Christian love? It is a powerful, radiant and life-giving emotion, charged with extra-ordinary power both to the one who learns to love and the one who is loved. To some people, this great love comes as a free gift from God, but most of us need to learn it. And how can one learn it? *By practice.*

IDEAS UNLIMITED

My husband has made at least a dozen trips to Ethiopia for ministry there in the past few years. It is a very long and arduous trip, as well as an exhausting schedule when he gets there. So I thought what can I do to cheer him up and give him a little "shot in the arm" when he's so far from home? The idea came to print up a succession of Scriptures and hide them in his suitcase, so they would be a complete surprise — a love gift from me and the Lord!

In his pajama pocket:

> *"I will both lie down in peace, and sleep; for you alone, O Lord, make me dwell in safety."*
>
> PSALM 4:8

> *"He who keeps you will not slumber, Behold, He who keeps Israel shall neither slumber nor sleep."*
>
> PSALM 121:4

In his vitamin bottle:

> *"A merry heart does good, like medicine….."*
>
> PROVERBS 17:22

> *"Pleasant words are like a honeycomb, Sweetness to the soul and health to the bones."*
>
> PROVERBS 16:24

In his kit with:

Hairbrush:

> *"…the very hairs of your head are all numbered. Do not fear.."*
>
> LUKE 12:7

> *"The splendor of old men is their gray head."*   PROVERBS 20:29

Mouthwash:

> *"I will bless the Lord at all times; His praise shall continually be in my mouth."*
> PSALM 34:1

Sunlotion:

> *"You anoint my head with oil; my cup runs over."*
>
> PSALM 23:5

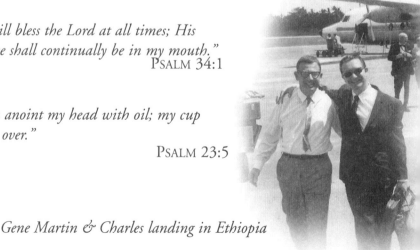

Gene Martin & Charles landing in Ethiopia

In his socks:

> *"How beautiful are the feet of those who preach the gospel of peace, Who bring glad tidings of good things!"*
>
> ROMANS 10:14

In his shoes:

> *"For the Lord will be your confidence, And will keep your foot from being caught."*
>
> PROVERBS 3:26

In his coat pocket:

> *"He shall cover you with His feathers, And under His wings you shall take refuge; His truth shall be your shield and buckler…"*
>
> PSALM 91:4

In his wallet:

> *"Beloved, I pray that you may prosper in all things and be in health, just as your soul prospers."*
>
> III JOHN v.2

Charles with orphan children in El Salvador

And a very special promise from Isaiah 58: 10-12:

> *"If you give yourself to the hungry, and satisfy the desire of the afflicted,*
> *Then your light will rise in darkness,*
> *And your gloom will become like midday.*
> *And the Lord will continually guide you,*
> *And satisfy your desire in scorched places,*
> *And give strength to your bones;*

And you will be like a watered garden,
And like a spring of water whose waters do not fail.
And those from among you will rebuild the ancient ruins;
You will raise up the age-old foundations;
And you will be called the repairer of the breach,
The restorer of the streets in which to dwell."

"But whoever listens to Me will dwell safely,
And will be secure, without fear of evil."

PROVERBS 1:33 NKJ

A BIGGER CHALLENGE

This "way of life" takes on a new dimension when it comes to loving our enemies. Sometimes it requires our forgiveness of others.

It was August, 1976, that my husband faced charges of fraud in the sale of securities in conjunction with building a hospital known as Life Center. The Grand Jury voted that he must stand trial. As I sat in the courtroom for those two long weeks, listening to the many vitriolic accusations against my husband, I was faced with some angry emotions and struggled with just how to overcome them. Then I remembered Jesus' words:

"Blessed are you when men revile you, and persecute you, and say all kinds of evil against you falsely…love your enemies, and pray for those who persecute you."

MATTHEW 5:11, 44

So I decided to do just that — "see them in God" — as a friend advised, praying for the District Attorney, the prosecuting Attorney, the Jury and even the Bailiff. I am so grateful that God gave me the opportunity to pray at that very time because three of those persons met death not long after — some of them experiencing a very tragic end.

In that same period of time we returned home one day to find a note pinned to our front door:

"We don't want crooks in our neighborhood. Please move!"

It was unsigned, and of course I wondered which neighbor it might be. Soon after, while shoveling snow from our front walk, I decided to include the walks of my neighbors on both sides, praying for them as I did so. I don't know how that little act was received, but as for me, I know my own heart was filled with joy and peace as I learned forgiveness, "returning good for evil," just in case.

"We don't have to furnish the love, we only have to choose for it to outflow. Through union with Jesus, the love is given — we only have to pass it on." (Rufus Moseley) [7]

The avenues are unlimited. Each day is filled with a multitude of opportunities within our reach. When the *way of love* becomes our *way of life*, we become conduits of God's love. And He so much wants us to learn this lesson in love, that He will allow unlimited situations in order to prove the experiment. Then life becomes a continuous succession of thrills. You will have a book of your own to write!

I can never forget that happy little man, Charlie Osborne, a Catholic layman, who spoke at our church some years ago. After his conversion he adopted the "way of LOVE" for his way of life and the stories were unbelievable of the many he led to Christ as a result. When he offered the bill of sale to the thief who stole his airplane, and said to him: "Here, keep it — you must need it more than I do." Believe me! That man left an impression!

NO ROOM FOR FEAR

"There is no fear in love; but perfect love casteth out fear."

I JOHN 4:18 KJ

"Fear is the painful emotion that arises at the thought that we may be harmed or made to suffer. This fear persists while we are subject to the will of someone who does not desire our well-being. The moment we come under the protection of one of good will, FEAR IS CAST OUT. A child lost in a crowded store is full of fear because it sees the strangers around it as enemies. In its mother's arms a moment later all the terror subsides. The known good will of the mother casts out fear.

The world is full of enemies, and as long as we are subject to the possibility of harm from these enemies, fear is inevitable. The effort to conquer fear without removing the causes is altogether futile. As long as we are in the hands of chance, or as long as we look for hope to the law of averages, as long as we must trust for survival to our ability to outthink or outmaneuver the enemy, we have every good reason to be afraid. And *"fear hath torment."*

To know that LOVE IS OF GOD and to enter into the secret place leaning upon the arm of the Beloved — THIS, AND ONLY THIS CAN CAST OUT FEAR. Let a man become convinced that nothing can harm him and instantly for him *all fear goes out* of the universe. The nervous reflex, the natural revulsion to physical pain may be felt sometimes, but the deep torment of fear is gone forever – because GOD IS LOVE AND GOD IS SOVEREIGN! [8]

His LOVE disposes Him to desire our everlasting welfare and His SOVEREIGNTY enables Him to secure it. Nothing can hurt a good man." — A. W. Tozer

> *"Keep yourselves in the love of God."*
> *Jude 2*

> *The body they may kill:*
> *God's truth abideth still,*
> *His kingdom is forever.*
>
> "A Mighty Fortress" Martin Luther

Now we begin to understand how *"perfect love casts out fear."* We do not have to try to get rid of it — it's the automatic effect of a love-filled heart. It's like light and darkness. They cannot co-exist in the same place at the same time. The songwriter said it well:

> *"LOVE will teach us how to pray,*
> *LOVE will drive the gloom away,*
> *Turn our darkness into day — When LOVE shines in."*

PERFECT LOVE! IT'S THE PERFECT ANTI-DOTE TO FEAR!

2
VICTIM OR
VICTOR?

What are you haunted by? And we say — "By nothing."

This question posed by one author caused me to stop and think a moment. Can this be true?

But the truth is that we are all haunted by something. It might be a secret sin — a hidden fear — a past failure or mistake – or even a present experience. We are sometimes, if not often, driven by these inward churnings — even totally unaware of how they affect our behavior. But the enemy of our soul takes great delight in diverting our attention, diluting our energy, filling our lives with doubtfulness and uncertainty, causing us to flounder and wander aimlessly — thus robbing us of God's best for our life.

The Psalmist says in Psalm 25 that we are to be haunted by the Lord — the whole of our life inside and out is to be absolutely dominated by the presence of God. Just as a child is so mother-haunted that although he is not consciously thinking of his mother, yet when calamity arises, the relationship that abides is that of the mother. So we are to live and move and have our being in God, to look at everything in relation to God, because the abiding consciousness of God pushes itself to the front all the time.[1]

If we are governed by God, nothing else can get in – no cares, no tribulation, no anxieties, no FEARS. How can we dare be so utterly unbelieving when God is round about us? To be controlled by God is to have an effective barricade against all the onslaughts of the enemy.

And to this man is promised: *"His soul shall dwell at ease."* – Psalm 25:13

In tribulation, misunderstanding, slander, turmoil — in the midst of all these things, if our life is hid with Christ in God, He will keep us at ease. IF GOD IS OUR REFUGE — NOTHING CAN COME THROUGH THAT SHELTER!

The secret is — **SEEING GOD IN EVERYTHING!**

This was the secret of Joseph's life. (Genesis 37-50) Time and time again you will notice how he related to God.

When he was tempted to sin with Potiphar's wife he didn't say, "I must not sin against her;" he said, " I cannot do this great sin *against God.*"

When he was asked to interpret Pharoah's dream, he didn't say, "I have the answer." He said, "I do *not* have the answer, but *God* will give it to me."

When his brothers came and they were so fearful he would take revenge on them, Joseph said, *"It was not you who caused me to be here. It was God that sent me before to preserve life."* He even requested, "Go back and tell my father Jacob, God has exalted me to this position and made me lord over all of Egypt."

At the birth of his sons Joseph didn't say, "I have two sons"; he said, *"God made me fruitful in order to make me forget all my sorrow."*

It's no wonder that even the ungodly Pharoah exclaimed, *"Is there a man like this in whom we can find a divine spirit?"* It was because Joseph saw God in everything.

This is not easy. It isn't natural. We don't usually view life this way. Only the Holy Spirit can enable us to perceive circumstances from God's viewpoint. I can remember my husband saying to me in one of the darkest moments of his life, "I will be so glad when this trouble is over and we can get this show on the road again." Then, he said, that I looked at him rather thoughtfully and replied, "Darling, *I think this is the show!"*

It's so easy to blame men — or the devil; we don't look for God's purposes in the midst of our suffering. And we almost miss it! Because sometimes the greatest thing He does for us is that which He does *in* us.

HEROES AND HEROINES

Many are the stories of faith and courage that have been told since 9-11. (It is reported that there are at least 900 new authors since then.) But the message that comes through loud and clear is this:

THERE IS NO FORTITUDE LIKE THAT OF FAITH!

And faith seems to shine the brightest in the dark night of tragedy and suffering. We see it on the countenance and in the words of Lisa Beamer, whose husband, Todd, was one of the heroes of Flight 93, which crashed in Pennsylvania: She writes in her book, "Let's Roll:"

"Todd and I always believed we're here to build a relationship with God and to build an eternity with Him. That has not changed at all. In God's wisdom, He allowed this to happen for Todd. It doesn't mean I'm happy about it, but I can accept it more easily." [2]

Here is a faith that sees the invisible — that looks beyond her tears to the future that God has promised to those who trust in Him. Just like the heroes and heroines of Hebrews 11, both she and Todd have *embraced the promises, confessing that they were strangers and pilgrims on the earth, now desiring a better, that is, a heavenly country. Therefore God is not ashamed to be called their God, for He has prepared a city for them.* Hebrews 11:13-16.

When the two unknown American missionaries, Dayna Curry and Heather Mercer, were rescued from a Taliban prison in Afghanistan, they were asked the question: What was it like in prison? They each replied:

Mercer: "I did a study in the book of Acts, and…I could see that persecution was actually the catalyst for growth in the church. While reading about Paul's suffering, I was thinking, "How can I get out of this place?" Yet Paul was asking, "How can my imprisonment build the church?

God really brought some revelation to me about persecution. We sang… *There is a Light in the Darkness*…a song of intercession for the Afghan people and…of peace in the midst of literal darkness. The electricity is out, I'm lying in bed, there are bombs going off everywhere, and I'm singing, *There is a Light in the Darkness and His name is Jesus.* That was powerful!"

Curry: " I read the Psalms every day — that…really put things in perspective and encouraged me to have a more thankful heart." [3]

Who are these brave and courageous people? Where have they come from?

They are those who have taken His precepts for their rule and His promises for their portion. Who, having taken God to be *their God,* stand in awe of his majesty and worship Him with reverence, submit to His authority and obey Him with cheerfulness. These are "His people — His friends." No wonder they are able to sing with the Psalmist:

> *"The Lord is my Light and my Salvation,*
> *Whom, shall I fear?*
> *The Lord is the Strength of my life; of whom, shall I be afraid?*
> *Though an host should encamp against me, my heart shall not fear:*
> *though war should rise against me, in this will I be confident.*
> *For in the time of trouble he shall hide me in his pavilion: in the secret*
> *of his tabernacle shall he hide me; he shall set me upon a rock.*
> *And now shall mine head be lifted up above mine enemies round about me:*
> *therefore will I offer in His tabernacle sacrifices of joy; I will sing, yea, I*
> *will sing praises unto the Lord."*
>
> PSALM 27:1, 3, 5, 6 KJ

These stories are reminiscent of those heroes and heroines of faith in Hebrews 11. There were not only those who were *"valiant in fight,"* those who *"escaped the edge of the sword,"* those who *"out of weakness were made strong,"* and who *"had trial of cruel mockings and imprisonment,"* but also those who *"were tortured, not accepting deliverance; that they might obtain a better resurrection."*

The same faith that delivers some from death enables others to die victoriously.

Faith is not a bridge over troubled waters, but is a pathway through them. And that "hall of fame" chapter concludes with these triumphant words:

*"And these all, having obtained a good report through faith...
that **God had provided some better thing.**"* VERSES 39-40

I love the way Psalm 25:12 is translated in THE MESSAGE:

*"**My question:** What are God worshipers like?
Your answer: Arrows aimed at God's bull's eye."*

MORE THAN CONQUERORS

The enemies have sometimes confessed themselves baffled and overcome by the invincible courage and constancy of those who have been victims of tragedy and loss. But when we believe those triumphant words of the Apostle Paul to the Romans, we can be not only conquerors, but *more than conquerors*, that is, *triumphers*. Those are more than conquerors that conquer.

In the Greek the word is "hupernikao." From huper, "over and above," and nikao, "to conquer." The word describes one who is *super victorious*, who wins more than an ordinary victory, but who is overpowering in achieving abundant victory. This is not the language of conceit, but of confidence. Christ's love conquered death, and because of His love, we are **hupernikao!**

I can never forget the message preached from our pulpit many years ago by Esther Kerr Rusthoi entitled, "More Than Conquerors." The thrust of it has remained in my heart:

When that which was meant to destroy us becomes a stepping stone to greater thingss – then we are "more than conquerors."

Incidentally, it was she who penned the words to that beloved song:

WHEN WE SEE CHRIST
Oft-times the day seems long, our trials hard to bear,
We're tempted to complain, to murmur and despair;
But Christ will soon appear to catch His Bride away,
All tears forever over in God's eternal day.
It will be worth it all when we see Jesus,

Life's trials will seem so small when we see Christ;

One glimpse of His dear face all sorrow will erase,

So bravely run the race till we see Christ. [4]

THE LOVE THAT WILL NOT LET US GO

In his letter to the Romans, chapter 8, Paul goes on with a poet's fervor and a lover's rapture to sing of how nothing can separate us from the love of God in our Risen Lord. He defiantly and triumphantly raises *five unanswerable questions* designed to give believers a profound assurance of spiritual security.

"What then shall we say to these things? (v.31)

If God is for us, who can be against us? *(v.31)*

He who did not spare His own Son, but delivered Him up for us all,

How shall He not with Him also freely give us all things?

Who shall bring a charge against God's elect?

It is God who justifies.

Who is he who condemns?

It is Christ who died, and furthermore is also risen,

Who is even at the right hand of God

Who also makes intercession for us.

"Who shall separate us from the love of Christ?

Shall tribulation, or distress, or persecution, or famine, or nakedness, or peril, or sword?

As it is written, For your sake we are killed all the day long;

We are accounted as sheep for the slaughter.

*Yet, in all these things we are **more than conquerors** through Him who loved us.*

For I am persuaded, that neither death, nor life, nor angels, nor principalities, nor powers, nor things present, nor things to come, nor height, nor depth, nor any other created things, shall be able to separate us from the love of God, which is in Christ Jesus our Lord."

ROMANS 8:31-39 NKJ

In the words of Barclay, the Greek scholar:

"With one tremendous leap and adventure of thought, Paul has seen Christ, not as the Judge, but as the lover of the souls of men.

No affliction, no hardship, no peril can separate us. (v.36) Though the world be falling about our ears, we can still have sweet times with Christ. The disasters of the world do not separate a man from Christ; they bring him closer yet. In verses 38 and 39 Paul makes a list of terrible things. Neither life nor death can separate us from Christ. In life we live with Christ; in death we die with Him; and because we die with Him, we also rise with Him; and death, so far from being a separation, is only a step into His nearer presence. Death is not the end; it is only 'the gate on the skyline' leading to the presence of Jesus Christ.

Here is a vision to take away all loneliness and all fear. Paul is saying: "You can think of every terrifying thing that this or any other world can produce. Not one of them is able to separate the Christian from the love of God which is in Jesus Christ, who is '*Lord of every terror* and *Master of every world.*' Of what then shall we be afraid?" [5]

NEITHER THE SENSE OF* TROUBLES PRESENT, *NOR THE FEAR OF* TROUBLES TO COME *CAN SEPARATE US FROM THAT KIND OF LOVE.

BELIEVE IT. RECEIVE IT. AND SAY...

"GOOD-BYE TO FEAR!"

NOTES

Part I
Chapter One
1 Denver Post, Oct. 14, 2001
2 Wall Street Journal, Oct. 19, 2001
3 "The Meaning of Prayer," – Fosdick
Chapter Two
1 Spirit-Filled Bible, Commentary on Job
2 "Knowing God" – J. I. Packer, 1973, Intervarsity Press, p. 23

Part II
Chapter Two
1 "None of These Diseases" – S. I. McMillan, Revell
Chapter Four
1 "On Eagles' Wings" – 1991, New Dawn Music
2 "The Hiding Place" – 1971, Chosen Books, p. 67
Chapter Five
1 "Through It All" – Andrea Crouch, 1971, MANNA MUSIC, INC
2 "Table in the Wilderness" – 1978, Tyndale, March 2, Jan. 25
3 "Table in the Wilderness" – 1978, Tyndale, March 21
4 "Press On" – Dan Burgess, 1983, Good Life Publications
Chapter Six
1 "Shepherd of Love" – 1966, John Peterson Music Co.
2 "I Think It Harder" – Poem, Ruth Bell Graham
3 "I Know Who Holds Tomorrow" – 1950, Ira Stanphill, Benson Pub.

Part III
Chapter One
1 "Love or Perish" – Dr. Smiley Blanton, 1955, Simon & Schuster
2 "Perfect Everything" – Rufus Moseley, 1952, Macalester Park Pub.-p.69
3 "My Tribute" – Andre' Crouch, 1971, Lexicon
4 "The Normal Christian Life" – Watchman Nee, 1964, p. 166
5 "The Unshakable Kingdom & the Unchanging Person" – E.S.Jones, 1972, Abingdon Press, p. 94
6 "The Blessing" – Gary Smalley, 1986, Thomas Nelson, Chapter 2
7 "Perfect Everything" – Rufus Mosley, 1952, Macalester Park Pub.-p.72
8 "Knowledge of the Holy" – A. W. Tozer, 1961, Harper & Row

Chapter Three
1 "My Utmost For His Highest" – O. Chambers, Barbour Pub. 1963, June 2
2 "Let's Roll" – Lisa Beamer, Tyndale, 2002
3 "Angels in Afghanistan" – CHARISMA, Sept., 2002, p. 38
4 "When we see Christ"– Esther Kerr Rusthoi, 1941, Singspiration, Inc.
5 "Letter to the Romans" – Wm. Barclay, 1957, Westminster Press, p.123

RESEARCH SCRIPTURE
New American Standard, 1975, Holman Co.
New King James, Spirit Filled Bible – 1991, Thomas Nelson
Dakes Study Bible – 1963, Dakes Bible
Thompson Chain Reference – 1964, Kirkbride Bible
Authorized King James 1611

By purchasing this book, you are

ANSWERING *the* ETHIOPIAN CALL

In a letter from the President of the Benishangul–Gumuz region of Ethiopia, he pleads for help –

"As a practicing Christian, I attach great importance to the role the gospel of our Lord and Savior Jesus Christ can play in promoting the peace and development efforts of the region. I believe I am here for such a time like this, i.e., to turn the history of the region towards peace and prosperity through the liberating power of God."

He believes that if a church can be planted in one third of the villages (1,000), the rest of the region will be evangelized. He truly feels that in the history of humanity there has never been such an opportunity as this.

The heart of my husband has been moved to tirelessly rally an effort far and wide to help meet this challenge, and I want to be a part as well. Therefore, the proceeds from this publication will be used for this cause.

To learn more about establishing an Ethiopian church in your name, or as a memorial to someone you love, contact me at: ceb@blairfoundation.com or

Betty Blair

P. O. Box 9950,

Denver, CO 80209.

Photo on left: Charles with President Yaregal Aysheshim of the Gumuz region of Ethiopia. *Photo on right:* a church in Ethiopia. *Bottom right:* Letter from President Aysheshim.